SUGGESTIONS

T0382365

SUGGESTIONS

LITERARY ESSAYS

BY

E. E. KELLETT

CAMBRIDGE
AT THE UNIVERSITY PRESS
1923

CAMBRIDGE
UNIVERSITY PRESS

University Printing House, Cambridge CB2 8BS, United Kingdom

Cambridge University Press is part of the University of Cambridge.

It furthers the University's mission by disseminating knowledge in the pursuit of education, learning and research at the highest international levels of excellence.

www.cambridge.org
Information on this title: www.cambridge.org/9781107505186

© Cambridge University Press 1923

First published 1923
First paperback edition 2015

A catalogue record for this publication is available from the British Library

ISBN 978-1-107-50518-6 Paperback

PREFACE

SOME of these essays have already appeared—in *The Quest*, *The London Mercury*, *The British Review*, *The London Quarterly Review*—and I desire here to make the usual acknowledgments. About half of them are now printed for the first time.

The title is deliberately chosen: for many of my opinions I do not expect acceptance, but it will be enough if they provoke thought and stimulate discussion.

I should like to tender special thanks to the officials of the Cambridge University Press for the minute care they have expended on a work which offers many chances of error in detail.

E. E. K.

CAMBRIDGE
September 1923

CONTENTS

I

Shakspere's Amazons

Behold, it is my younger brother dressed,
A man, or woman, that hath gulled the world.
FIELD, *Amends for Ladies*, III. 2.

THAT in Shakspere's time, on the public stage, the parts of women were played by boys is a fact too well known to require more than the very briefest reference. "Every schoolboy knows" that actresses were not seen in England, except in private performances, till after the Restoration[1]; and most people could tell us that on January 3, 1660 (old style), Samuel Pepys saw women on the stage for the first time. The dullest reader of Shakspere's plays never fails to catch the point when he lights on Rosalind's epilogue: "If I were a woman I would kiss as many of you as had beards that pleased me"; and everybody understands the Egyptian Queen when she says she will not go to Rome to see "some squeaking Cleopatra *boy* her greatness." Nevertheless it is less easy than one would think to keep constantly in mind the fact that the female parts were not written for a Sarah Bernhardt or an Ellen Terry, but for a Kynaston or a "child of the chapel"[2]. Many touches in Elizabethan

[1] The case of Davenant's *Siege of Rhodes*, acted in August 1650, is no exception. Though it is scarcely an opera in the real sense of the term, Davenant called it so to avoid the Commonwealth prohibition of stage-plays; and the women *sang* in it. They were, as Mr Schelling says, chosen for their voices rather than for their acting; and one of them, Mrs Coleman, had already appeared in a previous "entertainment" of Davenant's.
[2] The Puritan objection to stage-plays turned largely on the assumption of women's dress by men. Thus, for example, Rainolds, in his *Overthrow of Stage-Playes*, calls such an assumption "unscriptural"; and the same view is expressed by Gosson. No one would accuse Gilbert and Sullivan of Puritanism; but it will be remembered that one of their rules of action was never to give a man's part to a woman or *vice versa*.

plays are often misunderstood or passed over through a neglect, even momentary, of this point. There are some passages, for example, in speeches of Lady Macbeth or of Perdita which Shakspere would probably have written differently if he had meant them for the mouth of Mrs Siddons or Mary Anderson.

The chief complication due to this historical accident (for such it really is) of the English stage arises when a Julia or a Portia is represented as donning a man's clothes and mimicking a man's bearing and behaviour. We are thus confronted with the curious situation of a boy pretending to be a girl who pretends to be a boy. From the frequency with which this situation appears in Elizabethan plays, it would seem that the audiences were delighted with its piquancy, and had no objection to being thus twice beguiled—or rather to being, first cheated and then cheated of the cheat. At any rate the device is found half a dozen times in "Beaumont and Fletcher"; in *Philaster* for example, in the *Pilgrim*, in the *Maid's Tragedy*, in *Love's Cure*[1], and, very gratuitously, in *Cupid's Revenge*; while Ben Jonson's *Silent*

---

[1] *Love's Cure* is usually ascribed, wholly or in part, to Massinger. It is noteworthy that the device with which we are dealing is here much better prepared and motived than is generally the case in the genuine plays of "Beaumont and Fletcher"; and this fact is quite consistent with Massinger's authorship; for "the most striking feature of Massinger's art," as Köppel says (*Cambridge Hist. of Eng. Lit.* vi. p. 153), "is to be found in his great constructive power"; whereas the merits of Fletcher, unquestionably, lie anywhere rather than in his plot-construction. (Beaumont was dead before the earliest date to which the play can be assigned.)

Love's Cure supplies a specially elaborate development of the device. Here we have Lucio in woman's apparel, and his sister Clara, a sort of Bradamante or Britomart, in man's. The plot turns on Clara's sudden access of love for her father's enemy Vitelli, and its "humour" on a series of equivocal jests arising out of the confusion of dress. It may be observed that it abounds in obvious imitations of Shakspere: perhaps therefore it may be allowable to trace to Shakspere's influence the measure of skill with which the device is prepared.

The relation of *Love's Cure*, as well as of the *Pilgrim*, of which we shall speak later, to its Spanish original is well worth working out in detail.

Woman is based upon a variation of the same idea. Nay, the motive was a favourite with University playwrights, and presumably with their audiences. Not to mention *Laelia* (1595), a Latin setting of the story upon which Shakspere based *Twelfth Night*, we find in *Silvanus*, acted at St John's College, Cambridge, Jan. 13, 1596 (old style), the heroine Panthia assuming the disguise of man's apparel, and under the name of Erastus following Silvanus about like a faithful dog, while another girl called Florinda falls in love with her. So too in *Labyrinthus*, by Walter Hawkesworth (1603), Lepidus passes as a woman and Lucretia as a man; hence, says Professor Boas[1], arises "a bewildering and unedifying series of love entanglements before they are finally united to Lidia and Horatius, the son and daughter of Cassander"[2].

It must be remembered that plays of this class were among the greatest successes of their authors. The presence of this device was enough to excuse the total absence of any other merit. Even that miserable performance, *Cupid's Revenge*, to which we have already referred, is said to have been "often acted with great applause"; and it certainly passed through three editions. Indeed, the motive gave innumerable chances for introducing the touches in which Elizabethan dramatists and audiences delighted. Little "ironies" like Viola's

> My father had a daughter loved a man
> As it might be, perhaps, were I a woman,
> I should your lordship;

[1] *University Drama in Tudor Age*, p. 320.
[2] The appearance, in *Soliman and Perseda* (whether this play be by Kyd or by another), of Perseda "upon the walls in man's apparel" is hardly worth mentioning here. The whole scene of her disguise, if such it can be called, covers but fifty lines.

tiny capriccios, scarcely deserving to be called irony,
like Shylock's exclamation:

> How much more elder art thou than thy looks;

these, and a thousand others both delicate and indelicate,
must have "tickled" the Elizabethan auditor "not other-
gates" than a clever quibble in words, or than a confusion arising from the likeness between twins.

But—and here we reach the important point—it was
essential for that auditor not to forget that there *was* a
cheat. Precisely as, to use Coleridge's expression, he
must "suspend his disbelief," and allow himself—while
the play lasted—to be beguiled into thinking that the
boy was a girl, so he must *never* be allowed to forget
that, despite appearances, the girl has not—within the
"reality" postulated by the play—become a boy. Otherwise, the original illusion, willingly accepted by the
audience, would run a great risk of being destroyed
altogether. But this end was *at that time*, however easy
now, hard indeed to compass; for what in the play was
a pretence was in the actual world a reality: and the
acting, if *too good*, would be worse than bad. It is as if,
in the mock-play within *Hamlet*, the player-king and
his queen were to acquire a far greater actuality than
the Prince, Gertrude, or Claudius. *There*, however, a
few touches made all safe; Shakspere could, and did,
give to his "two-remove players" a wooden versification and a stilted style, while doubtless instructing his
actors to be even more wooden and stilted than their
style and their verse. So much so, that if we may believe

a story of Addison's, one of the worst of conceivable actors achieved a splendid reputation by playing the part of the Mouse-trap King so badly as to do it *well*.

But how was Shakspere to accomplish the far harder task of first making his boy a real Portia, and then turning Portia back into a boy who must not be so real a boy that we ever forget he is Portia all the while? It takes a god to perform the miracle described by Virgil:

> iuvenis quondam, nunc femina, Caeneus,
> Rursus et in veterem fato revoluta figuram:

but the miracle of a Portia is fully as difficult of performance. For the stage-conventions must not be strained too far. While the audience is to see that the doctor is the lady of Belmont, the doctor's part is to be acted with sufficient skill to make it natural that the Duke, and Shylock, and even Bassanio, shall not penetrate the disguise. The groundlings must recognise her all the time, but must never be led to cry out, "What fools are those people not to know her too."

To Shakspere, who, though the greatest of poets, was most emphatically a playwright, all these things were more obvious than to us; and he set about to conquer his difficulties in his usual commonsense and business-like manner. It was his aim to make things easy for his patrons; and he knew well that while audiences will put up with a great deal of obscurity or inconsistency in phrases or sentences, an awkward situation annoys them above measure. Hence we find that, like the old musicians preparing a discord, he always "prepares" his hearers for this situation with especial care. It may

be laid down as a rule that, in Shakspere's plays, a girl
who masquerades as a man either is, from the very first,
shown to us as of an even ultra-womanly character,
or else, *just before she assumes her disguise*, is represented in ways, or in circumstances, which bring her
femininity into a strong light. She is, in fact, either
an Imogen or a Rosalind. Not a single "masculine"
woman, in all Shakspere's plays, ever poses as a man.
But if we get a woman of strong character, she is carefully revealed at her most "feminine" just as she dons
the swashing and martial garb. Yet further, as opportunity offers, the audience is reminded, by hint or
gesture, of the "true" state of affairs—and that with an
iteration which is quite unnecessary on the modern
stage.

As one might expect, the skill with which this task
is accomplished varies between wide limits. Shakspere's
earlier plays are in this as in other respects comparatively
rude. In the *Two Gentlemen of Verona*, for instance,
the transformation of Julia is prepared both too carefully and not carefully enough. She is, it is true, feminine, but—unlike Imogen or Viola—not so obviously
and emphatically feminine that the audience, during
the time of disguise, needs no reminder of the truth.
The reminder accordingly is given; a preparatory scene,
of an obtrusive clumsiness which would by itself prove
the immaturity of the play, informs us of the coming
change. The dialogue with Lucetta is to the same pur-
port as that of Rosalind with Celia, but how different
in its effect upon us! And the same boisterous feeble-

ness characterises the later reminders: a few asides keep our attention awake, but with difficulty. "I grant," says Proteus to Silvia, "that I did love a lady, but she is dead." "'Twere false, if I should speak it," mutters the disguised Julia, overhearing him; "for I am sure she is not buried."

The case of Jessica in the *Merchant of Venice* is perhaps hardly worth detailed notice. She appears in boy's dress for a space represented by but a score of lines, and she vanishes with her lover and her father's ducats to re-appear as a thorough woman at Belmont. But we may observe that, brief as is her transformation, the fact that it *is* a transformation is carefully emphasised. She dislikes her apparel, and would fain keep herself in the dark: Lorenzo informs *her*, and reminds *us*, that she is "obscured" even in the lovely garnish of a boy. Here, however, Shakspere had better things to do, though of a like kind, in the same play, and it was not his cue to dwell upon the insignificant at the cost of the important. Yet we are ready, after Jessica, to expect a great advance, in Portia, on the crudities of Julia.

And a great advance indeed we find. The problem here is far harder than that of Julia, for Portia's mind is by nature more "masculine," she has far more of the intellect, the rationality, the courage, and the vigour which it pleases men, and Shakspere among them, to think the special marks of their sex. Here then, on that very account, Shakspere takes unusual pains to prepare us for the coming development. Shortly before the crisis of the play Portia, in her betrothal speech to

Bassanio, emphasises, even to exaggeration, her womanli-
ness: she is, she says, "an unlettered girl, unschooled,
unpractised"; and her words of surrender might befit
a patient Grisilda yielding to a Marquis Walter rather
than the masterful lady of Belmont whom we have
hitherto seen. Again, when she opens her purpose to
Nerissa, she exaggerates the change that is to come over
her. She is to prove a "pretty fellow, to wear her dagger
with a brave grace, and to practise a thousand raw
tricks of these bragging Jacks." None of these things
does she actually do afterwards; she wears no dagger,
she practises no raw trick. Why, then, are these boasts
put into her mouth—except in order that, by their very
exaggeration, we may be cautioned against being taken
in, even for a moment, by Dr Balthasar and his pains-
taking clerk? For a similar reason, half-way through the
trial, when she has conducted the case so skilfully that
we might be inclined to forget who she is, there comes
in that famous bit of by-play which sets us straight:
"Your wife would give you little thanks for that, if she
were by, to hear you make the offer"—a touch only
pointed and pleasing to-day, but in Shakspere's time
all but necessary. Nerissa follows with her contribution;
and then, the requisite effect having been produced,
Shylock's "We trifle time" recalls the husbands and
wives to their main business, and incidentally prevents
us, the audience, from wondering why the recognition
does not come now.

With Rosalind, who belongs (with Shakspere's usual
subtle differences) to Portia's class, the case is similar,

and the preparation similarly made. It is quite obvious from the first, for instance, that she is of a far stronger and—if we like so to say—more "masculine" character than Celia; and yet, just before the decision to disguise herself is formed, it is Celia that is, for the time being, the more forceful and man-like. Rosalind weeps because of the Duke's harshness; it is Celia that takes the office of comforter. It is Celia that proposes the journey to the forest of Arden, and Rosalind that shrinks from it. It is Celia that dares danger, and Rosalind that fears it. From that moment, it is true, Rosalind, despite her weakness of body, never fails to assert her strength of mind; but from that moment it would seem impossible for anyone to forget that for all the doublet and hose she is a woman through and through. Nevertheless, so careful is Shakspere to help the duller among the audience, that every now and then he reminds us, by one little ironical touch after another, of the "true" state of the case. "I could find it in my heart to disgrace my man's apparel and to cry like a woman," says Rosalind just as she enters the forest; and a hundred other hints follow in due course. On the other hand, a series of well-devised accidents excuses the failure of Orlando to recognise her, and delays the "anagnorisis" to its proper place at the end of the play.

Viola and Imogen, as we have already said, are altogether different. With them, the difficulty is not so much to keep their femininity before the audience, as to prevent it from becoming too prominent. Both of them are women *par excellence*—women, indeed, whom we can well believe Shakspere would have wished to be impersonated by women. Nay, it is not improbable that Viola at least *was* so acted on her first appearance; for everything seems to indicate that the first performance of *Twelfth Night* was at the court of Queen Elizabeth, and perhaps a private one, at which a maid of honour may well have sustained a part. Be this as it may, no one in the audience can ever have taken Viola for anything but a woman; and in the play itself the interest largely consists in watching how the revelation of her sex is constantly just avoided. To the Duke she all but betrays it on three or four occasions, and is only saved by a sudden turn in the conversation, by the entrance of the clown, or by some other fortunate chance. To Sir Toby and Sir Andrew she is on the very edge of confession, when Antonio enters in the nick of time, and the expected event is again postponed.

Nevertheless it is worth notice that even here Shakspere thinks it desirable to prepare us, by the dialogue between Viola and the sea-captain, for the coming metamorphosis. We see her *before* the change, and we see her making ready for it. For Shakspere's method is usually that of expectation rather than that of surprise: he desires us to say, "How is this, which I foresaw, being brought to pass?" rather than "I never expected that." Yet this dialogue itself is to be regarded less as telling us, "This boy-actor is a girl," than as saying, "This girl is really trying to be a boy." Her success is not great; but it is *just* sufficient to carry the weight of the plot. Much the same may be said of Imogen, whose pure and perfect maidenliness, indeed, must shine through thicker disguises than any that Pisanio can lend her. There is a strange pathos in the futility of her efforts to keep up the deception, which could in fact impose on nobody but those who, like Guiderius and Arviragus, were unsophisticated by the life of courts, and nourished in Arcadian simplicity. Yet even Imogen's change, slight and superficial as it is, is carefully prepared for us beforehand; and, when she enters as a boy, no one in the audience can for a moment doubt who she is.

All these little devices may seem trifles too light for a genius like Shakspere's; and our readers may well think that we are making too much of them. But, as a matter of fact, they are neglected by other dramatists, and those not always the weakest, even though they had Shakspere's example before them to teach them the right way. In Nathaniel Field's *Amends for Ladies* (1618), for example, the Amazon motive is employed with ridiculous profusion, and always to the bewilderment of the spectator. Without any previous warning, Bold appears "disguised as a woman"; Frank also appears in the same dress, and even masked, with nothing to let the audience know who he is; and Lady Honour, through about a third of the play, masquerades as an Irish footboy, again with not the slightest preparation for the change. One feels that, to make the plot at all intelligible, a placard must have been attached to the breasts of the actors, giving the necessary information.

At the end, one can only say, as Lady Proudly says to
Honour:

> 'Tis strange to see you, madam, with a sword:
> You should have come hither in your woman's clothes.

It is scarcely needful to refer to the pitiful instance
of Fidelia in Wycherley's *Plain Dealer*—a creature who
bears as much likeness to Viola as Voltaire's Pucelle
bears to Joan of Arc. Yet it may be noted that Wycherley,
working with *Twelfth Night* before him, not only de-
grades the purest of plays into the vilest, but also forgets
to follow it in those tiny technical merits which we might
have fancied would have appealed to him more strongly
than its higher and more imponderable characteristics.
Every touch of irony, every "preparation," is hopelessly
missed.

Field and Wycherley, though good craftsmen in their
fashion, are after all second-rate. But in this point the
Di Majores are no better. Even Beaumont and Fletcher,
playwrights assuredly of no mean order, and poets of
high rank, forget these principles, simple as they are.
They were, as we have seen, fond of the device of the
masquerading maiden, and used it repeatedly. In
Philaster, Euphrasia takes the name of Bellario, and
serves Philaster as Viola served Orsino. But her real
sex and name are totally unknown to the spectators:
she bursts in on us, to all intents and purposes a real
boy, in the first scene of the second Act, not a word
having prepared us for her; and all we can say as the
play proceeds is, "Who and what *is* this boy?" Both
her language and Philaster's, it is true, give hints as to

the real state of affairs, but the hints are thrown away, for the clue has not been provided; and a theatrical audience cannot, like the readers of a detective novel, turn back to see what points it has missed. Imagine the sayings of Rosalind or of Viola *without* their explanation present in the minds of the hearers! Similarly, in the *Maid's Tragedy*, Aspatia, the promised wife of Amintor, suddenly and without warning turns up "in man's apparel, and with artificial scars on her face"; but we learn this from the list of *dramatis personae*, and not from the play itself. An audience would need a sign-board to tell them who she is and where she comes from. The same, more or less, is the case with Urania in *Cupid's Revenge*[1].

As for Jonson's *Silent Woman*, it is a play depending on surprise, and working therefore by different laws from those which Shakspere usually followed[2]. Nevertheless it illustrates our contention in its own way. The curious anecdote told about its production in 1776 is

[1] In the *Pilgrim*, the hint as to the coming change of Alinda into a boy is perhaps plainer than usual. This play, which was produced in 1621, shows, we think, more marks of the influence of Shakspere than any other of Fletcher's; and, if Fletcher collaborated with Shakspere in *Henry VIII* and the *Two Noble Kinsmen*, it may well owe some of its merits to the teachings of the master. As is well known, it enjoyed great popularity in the seventeenth century. It was revised by Vanbrugh in 1700, additions were made by Dryden, and Dryden's last prologue and epilogue were those written for this performance. Alinda was subsequently acted with great success by Mrs Oldfield. The *Pilgrim*, in fact, is one of the few plays of the "Amazon" class, apart from those of Shakspere, that would not suffer in the hands of actresses. But its appeals to the gross taste of the vulgar mark all too clearly the real source of its interest and popularity. It is said by some to be derived from Lope de Vega; but its actual debt to him, even in respect to incident, is trifling, and, in respect to construction, nil. We have to seek elsewhere than in Spain for the origin of its unusual power.

[2] It is far from our intention to depreciate the surprise-drama: it has its great and distinctive merits; and in the hands of a master can be made very effective. But we think it will be agreed that it belongs to a lower class than the expectation-drama; and it is certain that Shakspere, like the great Greeks, preferred to write on the principles of the latter.

very much to the point. "The managers," says Gifford,
"most injudiciously gave the part of Epicene to a
woman; so that when she threw off her female attire
in the last act, and appeared as a boy, the whole cunning
of the scene was lost, and the audience felt themselves
rather trifled with than surprised." It may have been
for a similar reason that Pepys thought *Philaster* a
"mighty poor play"; for it too demands, fully as much
as *Epicene*, a male actor. Nothing, in any case, could
show more clearly the importance of keeping steadily
in mind the fact that the Elizabethan dramatists did not
write their female parts for women; and nothing could
show more clearly the superiority of Shakspere to his
nearest rivals, not only in all the higher poetic and
dramatic gifts, but also in the tiniest details of the playwright's art.

II

Some Medievalisms in Shakspere

SHAKSPERE is often so astonishingly modern that
we are apt to forget how much of his mental
equipment was medieval. When he was born, the
Renaissance had well begun, and modern science had
started on its way; but neither of them had yet forgotten
the rock whence it was hewn and the hole of the pit
whence it was digged. For example, the same Kepler,
who, just while Shakspere was writing the *Tempest*,
discovered the immortal Laws, believed in the Music
of the Spheres; and, the same Napier who, two years
before Shakspere's death, published the *Canon of
Logarithms*, was far more keenly interested in the
Number of the Beast than in exponentials. The Elizabethan age, indeed, was like the Bay of Melita—"a place
where two seas met"—and to understand it we have
to know the main currents of both. It is necessary
often, in reading the most trivial passages of Shakspere,
to bear in mind his double outlook; for more than most
men he was born "with large discourse, looking before
and after," forward into our age but also backward
into those that had preceded him.

We propose here to take three quite trifling, but none
the less interesting, examples of this medievalism. And

first, let us consider the well-known passage in the *Merchant of Venice* (III. 5. 78)[1]:

It is very meet
The Lord Bassanio live an upright life;
For having such a blessing in his lady,
He finds the joys of heaven here on earth:
And if on earth he do not mean it, then
In reason he should never come to heaven.

Many emendations have been proposed, that of Pope, "And if on earth he do not merit it," being perhaps the favourite. Aldis Wright, admitting the plausibility of this change, yet declares that "we rather require a word with the sense of 'appreciate'."

But in all such cases it is necessary to discover the general meaning of the passage before we begin to emend; and, on investigating this particular passage, we see that no idea of merit, or of appreciation, or of earning, underlies it. What it really rests upon is the idea of *compensation*—a very different thing. This idea has probably existed from the beginning of the world: it appears as Nemesis in Greece, and dominates the conception of Kismet or of Fortune elsewhere. If Polycrates is exceedingly lucky now, he will pay for it hereafter. Those whom the gods love are happy in their youth—and die before Nemesis has had time to punish them for their happiness. In the Middle Ages

---

[1] The following section was written quite independently of the article by Professor Skeat in *Notes on English Etymology*, p. 183. It will be seen that I agree with Skeat in finding an allusion to the well-worn medieval joke as to a married man's special chances of heaven; but I differ from him as to the sense of *mean*, which he takes to be the M.E. *menen*, with open *e*, to lament or moan. It is true that this word occurs in *M.N.D.* v. 1. 330, but I do not think that this sense, in the passage under consideration, is an appropriate one.

this idea was blended with that of the next world, in which, so it was thought, were to be found not only rewards and punishments for the virtues and vices of this life[1], but compensations and readjustments for differences of pleasure and pain among men below. It may perhaps have been a somewhat crude interpretation of the parable of Dives and Lazarus that gave either actual birth or wide acceptance to this doctrine; or the command "Lay not up treasures upon earth" may have been thus treated by some John Ball of very early times wishing to console his poorer hearers for their misery; but that the view existed and was strongly held is undeniable. Lazarus, having been poor on earth, is comforted in Abraham's bosom; Dives, luxurious on earth, is tormented in Hades at least until his totality of pleasures and pains approximately balances that of the beggar. It is plain to the most casual glance that the Gospel of St Luke lends itself very easily to an exegesis of this comforting kind; and the Epistle of St James even more so: "Hath not God chosen the poor of this world rich in faith, and *heirs of the kingdom which he hath promised?*"[2]

If Nemesis is to be propitiated, the lucky man must try to make himself less lucky while "fortune is merry."

[1] Such rewards and punishments were often most *naïvely* proportioned to the good and evil deeds. "ȝe seneȝeden," says God to the guilty in an *Old English Homily* (ed. Morris, pp. 230–41), "an ȝeur écenesse, and ȝe scule birne an mire écenesse. ȝe seneȝden alse länge alse ȝé lefede, and ȝe scule birne alse longe as ic lefie": ye sinned for your eternity, and ye shall burn for mine; ye sinned while ye lived, and ye shall burn while I live. This is the full doctrine of a medieval "Mikado."

[2] In the *Ancren Riwle* (ed. Morton, p. 216) this same doctrine is drawn from Revelation xviii. 6, 7: "Contra unum poculum quod miscuit, miscete ei duo: quantum glorificavit se et in deliciis fuit, tantum date ei luctum et tormentum." (The original Scripture is not quite exactly reproduced, but the interpretation is not affected.)

Not only Polycrates, but every wise man:

> Sperat infestis, metuit secundis
> Alteram sortem[1].

So in the Middle Ages, renunciation of this world's goods might secure good things in the next world. But besides that, a clinging misfortune, a thorn in the flesh, a nagging wife, might be looked upon as a guarantee of blessing in the future.

So familiar were these ideas that they passed from homilies into poetry, from Dan Michel of Northgate to Dan Chaucer. That thorough woman of the world, the Wife of Bath, knew them well. When she had made her husband in his own grease to fry,

> For angre and for verray Ialousye,

she adds the pious aspiration,

> By god, in erthe I was his purgatorie,
> For which I hope his soulé be in glorie.

January, in the *Merchant's Tale*, finds the doctrine somewhat of a trouble to him:

> I have, quod he, herd seyd ful yore ago,
> Ther may no man han parfite blisses two,
> This is to seye, in erthe and eek in hevene.
> For though he kepe him fro the sinnes sevene,

---

[1] Seneca, *Thyestes*, 612:

> Omne sub regno graviore regnum est:
> Quem dies vidit veniens superbum,
> Hunc dies vidit fugiens iacentem.
> Nemo confidat nimium secundis;
> Nemo desperet meliora lassis;
> Miscet haec illis prohibetque Clotho
> Stare fortunam, rotat omne fatum:

a passage which has probably influenced the Elizabethan playwrights more profoundly than any other in all Latin literature.

And eek from every branche of thilké tree,
Yet is ther so parfit felicitee,
And so greet ese and lust in mariage,
That ever I am agast, now in myn age,
That I shal ledé now so mery a lyf,
So delicat, withouten wo and stryf,
That I shall have myn hevene in erthe here.

His doubts are resolved when his brother Justin tells
him that his wife may not prove such a blessing after all:

Dispeire yow noght, but have in your memorie
Paraunter she may be your purgatorie:
She may be goddes mene[1], and goddes whippe;
Then shal your soulé up to hevene skippe
Swifter than doth an arwe out of the bowe!

There is no need to multiply quotations. We are
already in a position to understand the idea underlying
Jessica's words about Bassanio. In Portia, Bassanio has
a wife very different from her of Bath, and bringing him
as much happiness as poor January anticipated, but
hardly found, in May. He must expect, therefore, to
be paid out for this happiness in the next world: "in
reason," in all fairness, "he should never come to
heaven," a place closed to those who have been fortunate
here. How then is he to avoid the other place? Jessica
has no doubt about the answer; he must sacrifice some
of his present bliss, even as the votarists in a cloister,
according to Theseus, in order to be "thrice blessed"
hereafter, renounce the joys of the "earthlier-happy"[2].
Bassanio must be moderate *now*, lest he lose full

---

[1] This word we shall have reason to note hereafter.
[2] *Midsummer Night's Dream*, I. I. 74.

felicity *then*. In a word, he must "mean it"; *i.e.* as
Horace advised Licinius Murena to do, he must draw
in his sails and "diligere auream mediocritatem."

To illustrate the construction of "mean it" in such
a context is surely unnecessary. It is precisely that of
the phrase in the *Ingoldsby Legends*, "draw it mild,"
where *it* stands for everything, anything, or nothing.
"I cannot daub it further," says Edgar in *King Lear*:
that is, "I cannot continue playing this farce." "Lord
Angelo dukes it well," we are told in *Measure for
Measure*: "I wouldn't swank it so, if I were you," says
a London girl to another at the present day.

Thus the passage, as it stands in the First Quarto,
becomes perfectly clear, and no emendation of any kind
is necessary. If anyone prefers the reading of the
Second Quarto, or that of the Folio—both of which
retain the essential phrase *mean it*—we can have no
objection.

Our second example shall be taken from an even
better-known passage, the dialogue between Rosalind
and Celia in *As You Like It* (Act I. Sc. 2). As the two
girls sit and mock at Fortune, Celia observes that those
the "good housewife" makes fair she scarce makes
honest, and those she makes honest she makes very
ill-favouredly. "Nay," replies Rosalind, "now thou
goest from Fortune's office to Nature's; Fortune
reigns in the gifts of the world, not in lineaments of
Nature."

Now this distinction—that beauty and wit are *natural*,
while money and all our relations to our fellow-men are

matters of luck or chance—will probably seem to most people to-day a highly artificial one. A man's wealth, certainly, is quite as often inherited as his good looks, nor does an ugly man think himself anything but un-lucky in comparison with a handsome one. Yet this distinction runs everywhere through Shakspere. "Tell Olivia," says the Duke in *Twelfth Night*, "tell her my love, more noble than the world, prizes not quantity of dirty lands:

> The parts that Fortune hath bestowed upon her,
> Tell her I hold as giddily as Fortune;
> But 'tis that miracle and queen of gems
> That Nature pranks her in, attracts my soul."

Here the same idea holds sway. Olivia's beauty is due to Nature, her lands to Fortune. And so in fact every-where. It is Fortune that, as Shakspere complains in his *Sonnets*, provided no better for his life than public means which public manners breeds. In *All's Well*, Helena, brooding on her love for one far above her in wealth and station, says

> The mightiest space in fortune Nature brings
> To join like likes, and kiss like native things;

and later in the same play we learn that it is Fortune that had put so much difference between Helena's estate and that of Bertram. Nay, so familiar was the idea, that Shakspere could afford to allow Dogberry to go wrong on it; "to be a well-favoured man is the gift of Fortune, but to write and read comes by Nature." A statement like this to-day attracts no notice; but then it would seem to the dullest in the audience as absurd

as saying that two and two make five. Yet no one is
shocked by reading in the *Vanity of Human Wishes*
(line 319):

> The teeming mother, anxious for her race,
> Begs for each birth the *fortune of a face*;

a wish which, to Elizabethans, would have appeared
not only vain, but directed to a ridiculously wrong
address.

At the risk of being tedious we may remind the reader
that the idea is to be found *passim* in Ben Jonson. In
the *Silent Woman*, for example, when Cutbeard is
enumerating the impedimenta which cause a nullity in
marriage (Act v. Sc. 1), he mentions among them
"error fortunae," which Otter interprets as follows: "If
she be a beggar and you thought her rich." But the
antithesis between Fortune and Nature is brought out at
least twice in the same play (Act II. Sc. 2; Act III. Sc. 2),
the latter passage being much to the point, "We should
thank Fortune, double to Nature, for any benefit she
confers upon us."

Nor is this merely the modern antithesis, which is
seen so clearly for instance in our daily use of the word
fortune for personal possessions. It is *like* it, but not
the same; and we can, if we are careful, constantly
detect slight differences between the Elizabethan point
of view and our own. Take the famous lines in *Timon
of Athens* (IV. 3):

> Twinned brothers of one womb,
> Whose procreation, residence, and birth

> Scarce is dividant, touch them with several fortunes,
> The greater scorns the lesser: not nature,
> To whom all sores lay siege, can bear great fortune,
> But by contempt of nature.
> Raise me this beggar, and deny 't that lord:
> The senator shall bear contempt hereditary,
> The beggar native honour.

Here the very smallest consideration will show that the conception of Nature as opposed to Fortune is more clear-cut and distinct to Shakspere (if Shakspere it be) than it is to us. Otherwise the paradoxical use of "hereditary" and "native" loses all its force, and fails entirely of its effect. The whole speech is one long oxymoron, the point of which has vanished with the change in the connotation of the words.

But what we wish especially to emphasise is that the notion, true or false, is characteristically medieval. The first plain trace of it that we have detected is in that great teacher of the later Middle Ages—Seneca. Thus, in the forty-fourth Epistle, we find Seneca rebuking a correspondent, who had been complaining that first Nature and then Fortune had been chary of gifts to him: "Iterum dicis, malignius tecum egisse Naturam prius, deinde Fortunam"; and it turns out that Nature had denied the man good birth, and Fortune great wealth. In the ninetieth Epistle, again, occurs a passage which at first sight may seem strange, but which, on closer inspection, falls in with the rest. "If," says he, "the gods had made knowledge common, and we were born wise, wisdom would lose its chief virtue, namely that it is not among the gifts of fortune" (Si hanc quoque bonum vulgare fecissent, et prudentes nasceremur, sapientia quod in se optimum habet perdidisset; inter fortuita esset). That is, wisdom is not the actual gift of Nature, but the capacity for obtaining it *does* come from her. If all men were born wise, but in different degrees, their subsequent attainment of more or less would be a matter of fortune. The antithesis is the basis of many of those wearisome apophthegms which compose so large a part of the Senecan plays. In the *Medea*, for example, we are told (line 176):

>Fortuna opes auferre, non animum potest;

and innumerable other sayings of the kind might be adduced. From Seneca, directly or indirectly, the conception passed to Boethius, and, as was to be expected, it is repeatedly found in Boethius's philosophical pupil Chaucer. Not merely in direct imitations of the *Consolations of Philosophy* (as for example in the series of poems entitled *Balades de visage sans peinture*), but more informally elsewhere, does it emerge again and again in Chaucer's works[1]. It was Nature that gave the beauty to the "formel egle" in the Parliament of Fowls; and loveliness of body was her fatal gift to Virginia. "Allas," says the Host when the sad story is finished,

>Allas, to deré boughté she beautee:
>But yiftes of fortune or of nature
>Ben cause of deeth to many a creature.
>Of bothé yiftes that I speke of now
>Men han ful ofte moré harm than prow.

---

[1] In a note to the *Balades de visage*, which consist of a dialogue between Fortune and a complainant, Skeat tells us there is a similar dialogue in *Alanus de Insulis* between Nobilitas and Fortuna; obviously keeping up the same antithesis. As we shall see later, a great authority for the conception was the thirteenth-century schoolman

But the clearest expression of this distinction in Chaucer
is in the *Merchant's Tale* (E 1310), a passage borrowed
from Albertano of Brescia:

A wyf is Goddes yifté verraily;
Alle other maner yiftes hardily,
As londes, rentes, pasture, or commune,
Or moebles, alle ben yiftes of fortune,
That passen as a shadwe upon a wal.

It would be easy to follow the same thought down
through Chaucer's successors till we reach the time of
Shakspere. Suffice it here to point out how prominent
it is in the *King's Quair*[1], a poem which contains perhaps the most elaborate picture of Fortune and her
wheel to be found in English literature. Yet, while
King James ascribes—as a Stuart might well ascribe—
more power to Fortune than most other poets, he yet
conceives his lady's beauty as the gift of Nature, and
outside the domain of Fortune:

In her was jouth, beutee, with humble aport,
        Bountee, richesse, and wommanly facture,
God better wote than my pen can report:

Albertano of Brescia, to whose *Liber de Amore Dei* Skeat, following Köppel, refers
us for the source of a passage in Chaucer's *Merchant's Tale* (E 1311); as his *Liber
Consolationis* was the ultimate original of the *Tale of Melibeus*. Albertano himself
seems to have found some sort of basis in a text of the Book of Proverbs; but the
exact form of the doctrine is certainly not Hebrew.

[1] So too the author of the *Court of Love*, a close imitator of King James, bears the
opposition in mind (line 1121):

                O Fortune, cursed, why now and wherefore
                Hast thou, they said, beraft us liberte,
                Sith Nature yave us instrument in store,
                And appetyt to love and lovers be?

It is interesting to note that to Saxo Grammaticus the idea was equally present: "Hic
Amlethi exitus fuit, qui si parem naturae atque fortunae indulgentiam expertus fuisset,
aequasset fulgore superos, Herculea virtutibus opera transcendisset." Hamlet had
from Nature high birth, wisdom, beauty, intelligence; but the gifts of Fortune were
denied him.

Wisedome, largesse, estate, and connyng sure,
In every poynt so guydit hir mesure,
In word, in dede, in schap, in contenance,
That Nature might no more her childe avance.

A few further references may make still more clear
this medieval view of Fortune. The whole of the second
book of Boethius is devoted to the subject, and Chaucer's
poem on the theme is little more than a versification
of Boethius's didactic paragraphs. The old philosopher
directs his warnings against the "anguissous love of
havinge" (II. Metre 5): and in the preceding prose he
makes Wisdom say, "But what desirest thou of Fortune
with so grete a noise, and with so grete a fare? I trowe
thou seke to driv away nede with habundaunce of
thinges" (Chaucer's *Boethius*, Skeat, p. 39).

To Dante's famous discussion of Fortune a mere
reference is sufficient (*Inferno*, VII. 67 *sq.*). But we may
notice the opinion of Gelli as given in his commentary
on the passage (Vernon, *Readings on the Inferno*, I. p. 221):
Gelli

thinks Aristotle has written on the subject with more insight
than anyone else. He contends that the Aristotelian theory
is that the cause of all things that happen with regularity
or with frequency is Nature; whereas the cause of those
that happen rarely, unnaturally, or accidentally is called
Fortune. Riches, then, being so fleeting, so unaccountably
bestowed, and so rare, are as a matter of course assigned
to the capricious goddess.

In the *Romaunt of the Rose* (Trans. of "Chaucer,"
5403 *sq.*) there is a long passage on Fortune, and we

are not surprised to find stress laid on her special governance of riches and poverty:

> Men wene with hem they wolde abyde
> In every perel and mischaunce,
> Withoute chaunge or variaunce,
> Bothe of catel and of goode,   (5437)

but Fortune

> From her richess doth hem flee,
> And plongeth hem in povertee: (5471)

for she is "hir goddesse in poverte outher in richesse" (5490).

Thirdly, we will consider the speech of the First Citizen to Menenius in *Coriolanus* (I. I. 110), in reference to the latter's fable of the "Belly and the Members":

> The kingly-crowned head, the vigilant eye,
> The counsellor heart, the arm our soldier,
> Our steed the leg, the tongue our trumpeter,
> With other muniments and petty helps—

a speech to which Menenius retorts by calling the citizen the great toe of the assembly.

It hardly needs to be said that this is medieval, in the full style of medieval allegory. It resembles the symbolism of the Two Lights, the Sun and the Moon, on which so much of the argumentation between the Empire and the Papacy was based, or that other symbolism of the Two Swords, of which Christ said "It is enough," and on which plenty will be found said in the controversies of Dante with the Pope. The analogy of the body politic with the body physical is of course not only very old but very natural; but in the Middle

Ages it shared the fate of many analogies and was pressed to its utmost limits with scholastic thoroughness. As Taylor tells us (*Mediaeval Mind*, II. 276):

it was used to symbolize the mystery of the oneness of all mankind in God, and the organic co-ordination of all sorts and conditions of men with one another in the divine commonwealth on earth; it was also drawn out into every detail of banal anthropomorphic comparison. From John of Salisbury to Nicholas Cusanus, Occam and Dante, no point of fancied analogy between the parts and members of the body and the various functions of Church and State was left unexploited.

And similarly Gierke (*Political Theories of the Middle Ages*, trans. Maitland, pp. 22 *sq.*) tells us that

John of Salisbury made the first attempt to find some member of the natural body which would correspond to each portion of the State...Later writers followed him, but with many variations in minor matters. The most elaborate comparison comes from Nicholas of Cusa, who for this purpose brought into play all the medical knowledge of his time[1].

As, in fact, we read the medieval political treatises, we are reminded of the monkish work, *De partibus Virginis Mariae*, in which the limbs of the Virgin are tortured one by one into the most extraordinary mystical meanings. Some of the parallels, of course, are natural enough: that the head, for instance, should be the King is not surprising. The eye, again, might well be a sentry or a watchful magistrate, and the arm is easily supposed

---

[1] Gierke's notes and references (p. 132) are specially informing and interesting: *e.g.* he points out that to Nicholas of Cusa the teeth were the privy council, the liver the judiciary, and the stomach the grand council.

to be a soldier. But that the heart should be the counsellor or senator does a little astonish us; and it is
precisely here that we begin to suspect Shakspere of
medievalism, and to see that he is not drawing out a
symbolism of his own, but adopting one ready-made.
For, in the medieval writings on law or politics, it is
almost always *cor* or *pectus* that is *Senatus*. Take for
example the *Policraticus* of John of Salisbury—perhaps
the most representative of all these writings. Basing
himself, as he professes, on the so-called Plutarch's
Institutio Trajani, John writes as follows (*Policraticus*,
ed. Webb, I. 283, section 540 *c*):

Princeps vero capitis in re publica optinet locum uni
subjectus Deo et his qui vices illius agunt in terris, quoniam
et in corpore humano ab anima vegetatur caput et regitur.
Cordis locum senatus optinet, a quo bonorum operum et
malorum procedunt initia. Oculorum aurium et linguae
officia vendicant sibi judices et praesides provinciarum.
Officiales et milites manibus coaptantur. Qui semper ad-
sistunt principi, lateribus assimilantur. Quaestores et com-
mentarienses (non illos dico qui carceribus praesunt, sed
comites rerum privatarum) ad ventris et intestinorum refert
imaginem. Quae, si immensa aviditate congesserint et
congesta tenacius reservaverint, innumerabiles et incurabiles
generant morbos, ut vitis eorum totius corporis ruina im-
mineat. Pedibus vero solo jugiter inherentibus agricolae
coaptantur.

Here then we have the kingly-crowned head, the
soldier hand, and above all the counsellor heart; while
the slight differences between John and Shakspere tend
to diminish as we read the hundred odd following pages
in which the conception is worked out in fuller detail.

We even notice in a later sentence a suggestion for Menenius's gibe[1] at the "great toe of the assembly":

Pedes quidem qui humiliora exercent officia, appellantur, quorum officia totius rei publicae membra per terram gradiuntur. His etiam aggregantur multae species lanificii artesque mechanicae, quae in ligno ferro ere metallisque variis consistunt (Webb, II. 58, section 618 *d*),

while the way in which Shakspere's thoughts dwelt upon the symbolism is clearly shown in the famous passage in *Henry V* about the advised head that defends itself at home while the armed hand doth fight abroad:

Manus itaque rei publicae aut armata est aut inermis. Armata quidem est quae castrensem et cruentam exercet militiam, inermis quae justitiam expedit (Webb, II. 2, section 589 *a*);

and the Archbishop's speech on the honey-bees, though doubtless directly derived from Lyly, owes something to the same metaphor. This is not, of course, to maintain that Shakspere, like Chaucer, had studied John of Salisbury for himself; all we are here contending for is that, by some process of permeation or other, such medieval ideas as John expresses in a scholastic manner had reached Shakspere as part and parcel of the general intellectual equipment of his time. It may well have been some homily or sermon that formed the channel of transmission—just as, in a very probable view, stories like those of the "Cock and the Fox" came to the common people and to Chaucer through the sermons of Holkot.

---

[1] The pain of the workers is the gout in the State's feet (John of Salisbury, VI. 20). Is not "My foot my tutor" (*Tempest*, I. 2. 469), though due perhaps primarily to Lyly, traceable ultimately to John or another medieval publicist whose views were similar to John's?

Theologians of the type of Dr Shaw or Vice-Chancellor
Perne, preaching on politics as they so often did in those
days, may well have made the conception familiar; nor
is it the habit of preachers, when once they have got
hold of a parable, to refrain from pressing its details[1].

Bearing in mind, then, that Shakspere's view of the
body politic was identical with this medieval one which
we have sketched, we are now able to see a closer aptness
than we might have expected in the speech of King
Claudius to Laertes (*Hamlet*, I. 2. 45):

> What wouldst thou beg, Laertes,
> That shall not be my offer, not thy asking?
> The head is not more native to the heart,
> The hand more instrumental to the mouth,
> Than is the throne of Denmark to thy father.

This is not a series of vague and general metaphors,
but symbolism precise, definite, and technical: as
technical, in fact, as one of Donne's medical or scientific
similes. "The head" is the King as the crowned chief
of the State, Claudius himself; "the heart" is the
counsellor—it is indeed Polonius in his capacity as the
Burleigh of Denmark. The next line puts the same
thing once more, but with a slight alteration in the
symbolism. Claudius now appears as the "hand," that

---

[1] It may be desirable here to say that I do *not* believe in a Jewish origin of the idea
of the "body politic." In a note on the passage of *Coriolanus* which we are here considering, Aldis Wright remarks that of the ten *sephiroth* or Intelligences spoken of in
the *Kabbala*, the first, which is called the crown, is placed in the head, while the heart
is the seat of understanding; and every reader of the Old Testament knows that
"men of heart" are really men of brain, while fools are spoken of as destitute of
"heart." But, in the form the idea assumes in the *Kabbala*, there is every reason to
believe that it was the Jews who borrowed from classical authors, and not *vice versa*.
Though Jewish scholars may have helped to *spread* such notions, yet (whatever we
may think of the " Plutarch " on whom John of Salisbury professes to rely) the ultimate
source was certainly classical, and the method of developing it ecclesiastical.

is the King as soldier, who beareth not the sword in vain; while Polonius, who had just before been the senator or counsellor, takes now the allied character of the "mouth" or orator—a description which, so far as it can be earned by verbosity, no one, surely, ever better deserved[1].

[1] It is perhaps not too fanciful to compare here Milton's famous designation of the "corrupted clergy" as "blind mouths": gentry who, like Polonius, know how to talk, but in their lack of foresight prove very bad sentries. This explanation is at any rate far less fantastic than that of Ruskin in *Sesame and Lilies*. It may interest Baconians to observe that Bacon's idea of Fortune, as given in his Essays, is quite different from Shakspere's.

III

Shakspere as a Borrower

SHAKSPERE'S mind worked most easily when it was not troubled with the necessity of inventing a plot. Unlike some other geniuses, of whom among his own contemporaries Ben Jonson is perhaps the most conspicuous example, he was not only willing, but usually glad, to build on another man's foundation. True, as his powerful fancy realised the characters, they grew from masks into human beings, and generally transfigured the story along with themselves into something different from what it had been. True also, he loved to *combine* plots derived from others, and the interaction of the two plots often altered both. But the fact remains that the basal elements of his stories are, almost without exception, unoriginal. Sometimes those elements are supplied by an old play, sometimes by a well-known novel, sometimes by history. With the old play or the novel he usually dealt very freely; with "history," when it bordered on legend, he also allowed himself liberties; with historians proper, and especially with Plutarch, in whom he obviously recognised a spirit worthy of reverence, he kept himself within very narrow limits of divergence.

It is not always that these departures from the original are for the better. When taken under the spell of a high inspiration they are *always* so; but when they are made

at a point in the play where the flow of soul is for any
reason checked, they may be no better than what they
supersede. Samson, shorn and grinding at the mill, is
no better than his fellow-slaves. Thus, for example, the
fourth Act of *Measure for Measure* marks an obvious
decline in the interest of the play. Shakspere was
weary; and it is very doubtful whether, by the invention
of Mariana (if that can justly be called invention which
is but the repetition of the idea of *All's Well*), and by
the subsequent marriage of Isabella to the Duke, any
improvement is made on Whetstone's plot. The confused effect of *Troilus and Cressida*, again, may be
largely due to the alternation of adhesions to the original
with departures from it.

But it is on another result of this habit of Shakspere
that we wish here to dwell. Historians, dealing with a
subject familiar to themselves from long study, may
sometimes be observed omitting, by pure inadvertence,
important incidents or characters, and yet afterwards
referring to them as if they were equally familiar to
their readers. What they have read, they imagine they
have written. Novelists also, having plotted out episodes
in their mind, occasionally neglect to put them in their
place in the story, and yet assume that their readers
know all about them. The same phenomenon may, we
think, be observed in a few places in Shakspere; and it
is due to a like cause. Reading his old play, or his old
chronicle, he knows it—often almost by heart[1]. But as

[1] This might easily be shown, were this the place to show it, from the number of
verbal reminiscences of old plays in plays of Shakspere often totally unconnected
with them in subject.

he writes, he soon leaves it far behind; his mighty imagination carries him to heights immensely beyond the reach of his pedestrian predecessor. But sometimes, when perhaps his invention flags or his hand tires, he recurs to his original, it may be following it almost literally; and we find then that he may pass unnoticed some inconsistency between his own work and the old, or admit a reference to a point which, while clear in the old writing, has been left on one side by *him*. At other times, while still working on his own lines, and in the full tide of inspiration, he may actually *forget* that he has never mentioned the point at all. It is in his mind from the study of the old play; but his enthusiasm about the more important matters has betrayed him into oblivion of the less essential. In two words—there are times when, perhaps from mental or physical exhaustion, he fails to correct his original into due harmony with his own re-creation of it; and there are other times when, in the "proud full sail of his great verse" and greater thoughts, he neglects the trivialities of in- cident, date, and plot, even though the inferior artist who preceded him may have carefully marked them for him.

Examples may readily be found, though it is no part of this paper's object to prove them to be numerous. Still less is it our purpose to represent them as "examples gross as earth." One of our main points is that they *are* trivial: they may be spots, but they are spots in the sun; and they rather emphasise than diminish Shak- spere's true greatness as a poet. As a small but signi-

ficant specimen of the class, take the words of Hamlet
to the Queen towards the end of their fateful interview
(III. 4. 196): "I must to England, you know that?"
Hamlet's keenness of penetration is extraordinary; he
has already detected plots and thoughts as closely hidden
as this; but it is nevertheless noteworthy that no sign
is given as to the means by which he has discovered it.
As a rule we are shown his methods plainly enough; a
little playing with Polonius, a careful scrutiny of the
King, are his usual ways; but here we have had nothing
of the kind, nor has he himself so far mentioned his
suspicions. The Queen knows of the plot, but it has
apparently been kept rigidly secret between her and the
King, and is indeed only revealed to the Prince in the
third scene of the next Act. We are forced to conclude
either that Shakspere has altered the order of the scenes
as given by Kyd in the *Ur-Hamlet* or that, if the old
order has been retained, some lines have been omitted
in which Kyd gave us the requisite information. This
is not one of the slips which a man naturally makes in
a story of his own; but it is precisely one of those which
might occur when he is re-casting the work of another[1].

Or take a passage from a play somewhat similar to
Hamlet in its central idea. Whence the strong emphasis
laid on the death of Cicero in *Julius Caesar* (IV. 3. 178)?
Brutus says, "Therein our letters do not well agree;

[1] A mere reference here will be sufficient in regard to the strange lapse by which
Shakspere allows Ophelia to lend herself so readily to the plot to entrap Hamlet into
a confession. The point is dwelt upon by Sir Arthur Quiller-Couch in his *Shakespeare's
Workmanship* (p. 209): and his solution is simply that in Belleforest Ophelia *was* a
courtesan, and that in *his* narrative she plays, quite naturally, the part that in our
Hamlet seems so uncharacteristic. I doubt not that in Kyd she did the same.

mine speak of seventy senators that died, Cicero being
one"; and Cassius echoes in horror: "Cicero one!"
Cicero has previously been just mentioned in the play,
as a man of whom the conspirators had thought as a
possible member of their band but whom they had
rejected. To the hearer or reader of *Julius Caesar*, apart
from other knowledge, he is nothing. Why then is his
murder dwelt upon almost as emphatically as the suicide
of Portia? The answer is at once obvious when we look
up Shakspere's authority—Plutarch. In Plutarch Cicero
is of importance; and the effect of his death upon
Brutus is strongly marked:

"The triumvirs," says the biographer, "did set up bills of
proscription and outlawry, condemning two hundred of the
noblest men of Rome to suffer death, and among that
number Cicero was one. News being brought thereof into
Macedon, Brutus wrote unto Hortensius that he should put
Caius Antonius to death, to be revenged of the death of
Cicero and of the other Brutus, the one being his friend and
the other his kinsman."

And we are further told that Brutus grieved not more
for the death of Cicero than for the cowardly spirit of
the Romans, who could endure such deeds before their
eyes as ought to have grieved them to the heart from
the mere report. Now Shakspere knew all about Cicero
and the great position he held in Rome; but in the earlier
part of his play he had said nothing of it, nor later (amid
the excitement of composition) did he remember to put
down any account of the action that Brutus took to
avenge that great man's death. It was all familiar to

him from his reading; he omits to make his hearers equally familiar with it.

Somewhat different is the following. Bradley and others have called attention to certain apparently irrelevant remarks in *King Lear*, which only on the closest reading do we see refer to Goneril. Thus (II. 2. 38) Kent tells Oswald that he takes "Vanity the puppet's part against the king" and later (III. 2. 35) the Fool suddenly adds to a song the quite unexpected comment that "There was never yet fair woman but she made mouths in a glass." There has been nothing so far in the play to indicate that Goneril is especially enamoured of her beauty; and Bradley explains these passages as due to "carelessness," while hinting at the possibility that Shakspere may have shortened *King Lear* and, in doing so, omitted passages that might have explained these allusions. But it is noteworthy that in the old play, *King Leir and his Three Daughters*, from which Shakspere would conceive his first idea of Goneril, she is represented as particularly vain of her person, and as jealous of Cordella because of it. "Faith, sister," says she to Ragan (*King Leir*, ed. Nichols, p. 394), "what moves you to bear her such good will?" and Ragan replies:

"In truth, I think, the same that moveth you; Because she doth surpasse us both in beauty."

"Beshrew your fingers," answers Gonorill, "I tell you true, it cuts me to the heart."

In the lovers' descriptions of the two ladies, Gonorill is "lovely" and Ragan "princely." Again, Lear's mind

seems to dwell on his daughter's[1] love of finery
(II. 4. 267):

> If only to go warm were gorgeous,
> Why nature needs not what thou gorgeous wear'st,
> Which scarcely keeps thee warm.

Now in *King Leir* Gonorill shows this trait of character
very plainly. Speaking of Cordella to Ragan (p. 382),
she says:

> We cannot have a quaint device so soone,
> Or new made fashion, of our choice invention,
> But if she like it, she will have the same,
> Or study newer to exceed us both:

and later (p. 403), she makes it a ground of complaint
against Leir that he objects to her expenditure on dress:

> I cannot make me a new fashioned gowne,
> And set it forth with more than common cost,
> But his old doting doltish withered wit
> Is sure to give a sencelesse check for it.

Nay, so marked is this feature in her character that she
sneers at Cordella as likely to waste all her husband's
revenue on a single gown.

Now we would not omit to notice that a Goneril of
this kind might easily be made visible to the dullest
of *spectators* by a few touches of the actor's art; but as
things are to us *readers*, the fact remains that the characterisation in this respect is clear in the old play and only
obscurely hinted in Shakspere's: so much so that the
speeches of Kent and the Fool above quoted seem at

---

[1] It is not quite clear whether Lear is speaking specially to Regan or to Goneril, or to both: but apparently *this* part of the speech refers to Goneril.

first sight all but pointless or irrelevant. And the reason, in our view, is that Shakspere, having himself a full knowledge of the old play, forgot that his readers had not that advantage, and thus neglected to mark clearly for their benefit what was so obvious to himself.

All the commentators have noticed the parallel between Lear's curse on Goneril (II. 4. 160):

> Strike her young bones,
> You taking airs, with lameness!

and the passage in the old play (p. 406):

> Poore soule, she breeds young bones,
> And that is it makes her so tutchy, sure.

But they have failed to observe that the curse gains greatly in meaning if we assume that Shakspere's Lear, like the old playwright's Leir, knew or suspected that Goneril had already an unborn child. To pray God to strike with lameness a child already there is far more effective than to invoke a curse upon a child that only *may* come, and does not yet exist even in embryo. Similarly, the scene at the opening of the play is more forceful if we imagine that, as in *King Leir and his Three Daughters*, Goneril and Regan had been advertised beforehand of the King's question, and had *prepared* their flattering and somewhat rhetorical answers. In Shakspere's play they certainly do not seem to speak impromptu; but no Skaliger has been introduced to us as warning them to have their tropes and hyperboles ready.

Some critics have doubted whether or not Shakspere

had a novel before him in writing the *Tempest*. That the story, if there was one, must have altered much in passing through his hands is of course certain; that some touches in it were suggested by the recently-published narrative of Sir George Somers's voyage is also certain; but that for the main part of the story *some* underlying novel is to be assumed seems to us almost equally obvious. The source, indeed, may be ultimately the same as that assigned by "Monk" Lewis for his *Isle of Devils*, which Lewis declares to be based on "an anecdote in the Annals of Portugal." Lewis did not always tell the strict truth in such matters; but if that "anecdote" could be unearthed, we might be on the track of Shakspere's lost original. As the poem tells the story, Irza is shipwrecked on an isle haunted by demons, to which indeed only monks can approach unscathed:

Not India's wealth could make a layman land.

Here the girl is loved by the chief demon, who gives her not pig-nuts but gourds, but otherwise treats her much as Caliban promised to treat Stephano:

He showed her living springs, and noontide shades,
Spice-breathing groves, and flower-enamelled glades;
For her, he still selects the sweetest roots,
The coolest waters, and the loveliest fruits:
To deck her charms, the softest furs he brings,
And plucks the plumage from Flamingo's wings.

Be it, however, that Lewis's real source was but another "Sonnet from the Portuguese," the likelihood that Shakspere borrowed from a novel is no whit diminished. How else are we to explain the cryptic

reference to a good act of Sycorax, for which, though
a sorceress, she escaped death? "For one thing she did,"
we are told, "they would not take her life" (I. 2. 266),
but *what* she did is never revealed. Still more tantalising
are the two references to Claribel, the daughter of the
King of Naples, whose marriage to the King of Tunis
led to the tempest on which the whole story of the play
is based. We do not think it possible for anyone to read
these two passages impartially without seeing that they
imply a far clearer knowledge of Claribel's history than
the play itself exhibits. For the symmetry of the plot
they are either too strongly emphasised or not emphasised strongly enough: as we possess the *Tempest*
they might better be omitted; in the original story they
must have held a far more prominent place. Doubtless,
in fact, two or three chapters of that story were devoted
to a description of the negotiations between Tunis and
Naples, of Alonso's eagerness and Claribel's reluctance,
of the misgivings of the counsellors, and of the preparations for the voyage. Nothing less, surely, can account
for the persistence with which Sebastian "rubs the
sore" in Alonso's mind when the alliance has brought
disaster; and nothing less can explain the enthusiasm
with which, when the disaster gives place to good fortune, Gonzalo brackets together Claribel's marriage and
Ferdinand's. "In one voyage," says he:

> Did Claribel her husband find at Tunis,
> And Ferdinand, her brother, found a wife.

For, *in the play* as we have it, Claribel is nothing, and
Ferdinand all but everything. Almost as natural would

it be to end the *Merchant of Venice* with a paean of triumph about old Gobbo, as it is to end the *Tempest* in this fashion. But the secret is, that in Shakspere's mind, primed with the old story, Claribel *did* hold this prominent position, while, for reasons perhaps connected with the unity of the play, she fell almost entirely out of it as he constructed it. As has often been observed, the *Tempest* is almost the only Shaksperean drama that keeps the "Aristotelean" law of unity[1]. The Claribel portion, in such a drama, could only be alluded to. Had Shakspere been writing another *Winter's Tale* he might have given it to us in full[2].

Somewhat different is the case of the too famous dialogue between Henry V and the Princess Katharine. Something more than the germ of this is found in the *Famous Victories*; and must have made an impression not only upon Shakspere's mind but also upon that of his audience—an impression so lasting that, when they came to a play on the subject of Henry they fully expected a scene of the kind. Shakspere indeed, in the

---

[1] That law, as is well known, is not really to be found in Aristotle.
[2] I have sometimes been inclined, perhaps too fancifully, to think that the passage (*Tempest*, I. 2. 83):

> Having both the key
> Of officer and office, set all hearts i' the state
> To what tune pleased his ear,

may be based at second hand on the lines of Dante (*Inferno*, XIII. 58), where Piero delle Vigne says:

> Io son colui che tenni *ambo le chiavi*
> Del cor di Federico, e che le volsi
> Serrando e disserrando sì soavi
> Che dal secreto suo quasi ogni uom tolsi:
> Fede portai *al glorioso offizio*.

Perhaps the writer of the original novel was here quoting from Dante, and Shakspere copied *him* with variations. This of course postulates that the original story was written in Italian, and not, as some think, in Spanish, nor again, in Portuguese. But such tales are like Antonio's vessels; they travel to many countries.

epilogue to *Henry IV*, promised them to continue the
story, and to "make them merry with fair Katharine
of France"—a clear proof that he had the *Famous
Victories*, and that part of it especially, in his mind.
When the continuation appeared, therefore, the merry
scene of course is found in its place. But alas! in the
meantime Prince Henry has passed through a transformation in Shakspere's hands, as complete as he had
suffered in the popular histories. Falstaff is discarded;
the courses vain have been given up for ever; the
Henry of the old play has vanished, and the Henry we
know so well has taken his place. But the old play is
still before Shakspere, and the audience still expect the
promise to be redeemed. The dialogue must be given;
and given it is. How it lowers, for us all, the character
of the great King! Little indeed is there here of the
man who is "full of grace and fair regard," of the hero
whose "discourse of war is a fearful battle rendered in
music," or of the Admirable Crichton whose universal
attainments made the Archbishop think of miracle.
Instead, we have an almost typical stage-soldier, poorer
in mould than a Gower or a Fluellen, rough and com-
monplace, resembling a Marius or a Suvorof far more
closely than the "ideal man of action" whom, in the
view of many, it was Shakspere's intention to delineate.
Let us, however, cast a glance at the old play. There
we see a Henry who could woo Katharine as follows
(Nichols, p. 369):

> Tush, Kate, but tell me in plaine termes,
> Canst thou love the King of England?

> I cannot doe as these countries doe,
> That spend halfe their time in wooing;
> Tush, wench, I am none such,
> But wilt thou go over to England?

This picture, seen when Shakspere was thinking over the scheme of his Lancastrian series of plays, remained at the back of his mind. There it rested in oblivion as he felt the impulse of his "Muse of fire," and soared on the wings of fancy to compose the great choruses or to give us the Henry of the night before Agincourt, who could see the vanity of kingship and the "hard condition" that goes with a throne. But as the poetic glow faded— for even Shakspere had his hours of lassitude—the old scene came back to him: he re-read it; it provoked him to a lower kind of inspiration; and the result was a dialogue which is unintelligible except when we remember that it is really due not to the man of all time but to the unknown chronicler who gave us not the great statesman-soldier but the mere winner of the "Honourable Battell of Agincourt." Those who draw up "characters" of Shakspere's heroes, and seek in them consistent wholes, not unnaturally boggle at this scene. Some, indeed, calmly omit it from consideration; and they are right; for it is in the true sense not Shakspere at all. As well try to reconcile the Ulixes of Virgil with the Odysseus of the *Iliad*, as try to make one harmony out of the Henry of this play.

Much the same may be said of the somewhat similar inconsistency between the Hamlet who is lost by end-less deliberation and the Hamlet who sends Rosencrantz

and Guildenstern to their doom without a moment's
pause. The one is the Hamlet of Shakspere; the other
the Hamlet retained from the older story. As known
to the audience, the plot of the play *demanded* the
sacrifice of the two courtiers, and Shakspere could not
disappoint the groundlings by omitting it. But, as he
had worked over Kyd's earlier scenes, the Prince had
grown into someone very different from the avenger
whom no ghost could blame for dilatoriness; and thus
when Rosencrantz and Guildenstern "go to 't," we feel
a shock of surprise which we certainly do not feel in
reading the older versions of the tale[1].

It is rarely that Shakspere—at least in his later plays—
introduces a mere "accident"; that is, an advance in
the plot due, not to a development of character in his
heroes, but to an external chain of causation. When he
does introduce such a feature, he is careful to show the
influence of the accident *upon* the character of the hero.
But, unlike many great writers, he prefers the converse
way of working. Still more rarely is he guilty of the
weakness of telling us that such an accident has occurred, *without letting us know what it was*. So to do,
is to make a gratuitous and open confession of in-
sufficiency, it is to awaken the hearer's curiosity while
at the same time proving one's inability to satisfy it;
and usually Shakspere no more deigns such a confession than does a good novelist. When George
Meredith tells us that Diana Warwick crushed an enemy

---

[1] Dr Bradley's explanation of this incident is too well known to need more than
a reference. It demands, we think, the ascription to Shakspere of a certain modernity
of thought which is probably outside even *his* range.

by a witty sarcasm, he knows too well the rights of his readers not to give us the sarcasm in full; and a dramatist is still more bound to do the like. But on one or two occasions Shakspere, the greatest of dramatists and the keenest to consult the claims of his audience, fails to do so. We have seen already that in the *Tempest* he hints that Sycorax did *something*, but what it was he does not tell us; and we tried to suggest a reason. In the *Merchant of Venice* there is a more glaring case of the same omission. At the very end, we are all legitimately anxious to be "satisfied of events at full"; and a strange event indeed has just happened. Portia has somehow got hold of a letter which informs Antonio that three of his argosies have safely come to road. Everybody must wonder how on earth *she*, the least likely of all persons to chance on such a letter, has secured it: and we are put off simply with "you shall not know." This is not the Shakspere who prepares us beforehand by subtle touches for the melancholy of Jaques or for the fall of Macbeth. A sufficient reason must exist; and after what we have said our readers will be ready to guess it.

The *Merchant of Venice* is based on an old play called the *Jew*. The *Jew* is lost; but if we may judge by analogy, Shakspere did not slavishly copy it. His story follows its main outlines, even to the admission of the somewhat embarrassing casket-episode; but the greatness of the play, the sublime malignity of Shylock, the charm of Portia, are his own creations. As he fell more and more deeply under the enchantment of his work, he

left the *Jew* behind; and, doubtless, in the really inspired parts of his play discarded it altogether. In the
Jew, the means by which Portia acquired the letter
were probably fully explained in their proper place; but
that place was precisely one of those in which Shakspere was following his own spirit, and the incident
therefore passes unmentioned. But all plays, good or
bad, meet in their conclusions; and towards the end
Shakspere reverts to his "original." *Some* restoration
of Antonio's fortunes is obviously necessary; and Portia,
as the author of the *Jew* had seen, must be the agent.
But Shakspere now realises either that the actual means
by which she had secured the letter are absolutely inconsistent with the story as he has told it, or that he
must go back in cold blood and insert the explanation
in its natural place. Such reconstruction is impossible,
from want of time or of inclination. He therefore retains
the old narrative so far as to exhibit Portia's agency;
but explanation, whether borrowed from the old play
or invented *ad hoc*, is calmly omitted. That readers and
spectators usually pardon the omission, is due to the
strength with which Portia's character is put before us.
She "carries it off"; we feel instinctively that she is
capable de tout; but the omission is a flaw, slight it is
true, but a flaw nevertheless.

The same play supplies us with yet another example.
In the last Act (Sc. 1, line 33), we are told that Portia
is returning to Belmont with "a holy hermit and her
maid." At this hermit Johnson naturally boggled; for
"nothing is seen or heard of him afterwards." It may

well be that, as Johnson conjectures, the poet had first planned his fable in another way, and inadvertently left the line in when he recast it; but it may equally well have been the case that the original play, the *Jew* or another, found a use for this hermit which Shakspere's rendering of the story did not admit. In either case the oversight is but one more instance of the way in which Shakspere, rewriting the lines of himself or another, first ran beyond them and then, in a less exalted moment, returned to them.

We may next consider a somewhat remarkable example of the *negative* influence of the original authority upon Shakspere: of its effect, that is, in preventing Shakspere from carrying out a design *of his own*. Shakspere forms an idea in addition to those given him by his original; but, through following his original too closely in other parts of his play, forgets to develop that idea to its natural conclusion. *Macbeth*, it is well known, makes havoc of Holinshed in its earlier Acts, and reverts to him in the fourth. Now in the earlier Acts it is tolerably plain that Macbeth had at least one son. Lady Macbeth speaks of having "given suck" to a child; and the child was perhaps[1] a boy. Some people regard this boy as her son by a former marriage; but though, according to certain varieties of the Macbeth-legend, Lady Macbeth (or rather Gruoch) was a widow when she married Macbeth, there is no hint of this in Holinshed—who indeed only mentions her once altogether[2]—and not the

---

[1] The word *his* (I. 7. 57) of course does not prove this.
[2] "His wife lay sore upon him to attempt the deed ,as she that was very ambitious."

slightest indication that Shakspere either meant to use
the tradition or indeed knew of it at all. We need not
expect Lady Macbeth to be a Mrs Bayham Badger; but
some allusion to her previous marriage would have been
made—to speak truistically—had Shakspere concerned
himself with it. This child, then, is pretty obviously
Macbeth's. Later, we see further reason to think so.
What rouses the usurper's hatred and fear of Banquo
to madness is the realisation that Banquo's "issue" will
deprive Macbeth's son of his inheritance: the sceptre
will be barren, wrenched from him "with an unlineal
hand, no son of his succeeding." Bradley, it is true,
imagines that the King is here looking forward to the
possibility of a son. The other child is dead, thinks
Bradley; but King and Queen are both still young, and
may yet have many children. Admitting this latter statement as probable—for Macbeth's admiring "Bring forth
men-children only" (line 72) seems to lend colour to
it—we yet regard it as likely that the child referred to
is alive. Strong-minded as Lady Macbeth is, we cannot
think she would have spoken so ferociously, even in
such an adjuration, of a child whom she had lost. And
Macbeth's reference to his heir (though his exact turn
of phrase is perhaps more applicable to *heirs* than to
an heir) appears to us, on the whole, to confirm this
conjecture.

One argument against this conclusion, of course,
exists, though Bradley has deprived himself of it. Macduff's famous exclamation, on hearing of the murder
of his babes, "He has no children!" may certainly mean

"*Macbeth* has none for me to kill as he has killed mine," or, "Macbeth has no children, or he never would have brought himself to murder those of even his deadliest enemy." A parallel for the former view may be found in that favourite of the Elizabethans—Seneca. When Medea is planning revenge on Jason for the death of her brother, she says (*Medea* 125): "*Utinam esset illi frater*; est coniunx, in hanc ferrum exigatur"[1]. The second view is scarcely affected whether we regard Macbeth as *having*, or as *having had*, children. If the former be correct, the child is dead. Commentators seem fairly evenly divided on the question: Mr Scrymgeour, in his recent excellent edition of the play, says (p. 75): "Rather than permit Banquo's children to succeed—*Macbeth obviously has children of his own*, though they are not obtruded upon us—he is ready to enter the lists against fate itself"[2].

But whichever way we decide this point, at least one child has been born: and whether he has lived or died, a blank remains. No use is made of him. None knew better than the creator of Queen Constance that a mother does not forget her child. If he has lived, why does Lady Macbeth find no consolation in him? Why, even in that terrible void of her soul after the ghost-scene, does she not mention him even once? If he has died, still more why does she not recall him? Nothing could add to the superhuman power of the sleep-walking scene—except perhaps a reminiscence, surely almost

---

[1] As has been observed, the witch-scenes in *Medea* closely resemble those in *Macbeth*: compare also "ira quae tegitur nocet" (*Med.* 152) with *Macbeth*, IV. 3. 209.
[2] My italics.

inevitable in such circumstances, of the "clambering limbs and little heart that erred." "The Thane of Fife had children—where are they now?" would have been sufficient—but it is not said. The child appears, like that other child in Macbeth's vision in the cave, and vanishes equally suddenly, and equally never to return. "Come like shadows, so depart."

These negligences—if such they are admitted to be— like the confusion as to the date of Cawdor's rebellion, and like the unsolved enigma as to when Macbeth first broached the plan of Duncan's murder to his wife, are due, we can no longer doubt, to the alternating action of Shakspere's mind, now relying on its own unequalled force to create a passionate situation, and now, as the high frenzy leaves him exhausted, recurring to the original authority for aid. Under the one impulse he conceives certain ideas; under the other, as these ideas do not play a part in Holinshed, he forgets them. Just as, because the dialogue between Malcolm and Macduff *is* in Holinshed, he gives us that poor scene after the wonders of the third Act, so, because the son of Macbeth is not in Holinshed, he drops him as strangely as he drops the Fool in *Lear*.

The converse is the case with the disappearance of old Adam in *As You Like It*, just after he has been, with every circumstance of scenic interest, introduced into the presence of the Duke (Act II. Sc. 7); a disappearance so bewildering that some have endeavoured to explain it by the theory that Shakspere (who himself played the part), being a poor actor, and caring little for his task,

gave himself as little to act as he decently could, and
cared not how abrupt his exit might be. But the explanation is surely simple. Just at the end of *As You Like It*
we find a far wider departure from Lodge's *Rosalind*
than elsewhere, and Shakspere relies more than usual
upon his own invention. He has already, it is true, given
us in Jaques and Touchstone two *characters* of his own;
but here he alters *incidents* wholesale. The novel, indeed,
is cast entirely aside. Nothing is said of the rising of
the Twelve Peers of France against the usurper, or of
their march to the bounds of the Forest of Arden;
Duke Frederick is not killed, but—to provide mental pro-
vender for Jaques—becomes a "convertite"; Orlando,
unlike his prototype Rosader, is not definitively made the
rightful Duke's heir; and "Corydon" and "Montanus,"
who in the novel receive rewards, are passed over. No
wonder that, while thus trusting to his own resources
for the finishing of his story, Shakspere forgets that
Lodge had been careful to provide for the old age of
"Adam Spencer."

Our last illustration shall be from *Richard II*, a play
based almost entirely on Holinshed. As a rule, in this
play, the action is perfectly clear, and the history can
be learnt as well from it as from its authority. But in
Act IV the reader or auditor, unless liberally supplied
with notes, is inevitably bewildered. The scene in
Westminster Hall, with its accusations and counter-
accusations, on the part of people we have never seen
before, is an almost hopeless maze. Who is Surrey, and
who is Fitzwater? Why do they quarrel, and what party

does each espouse? The air, in fact, is full of gages,
flung by nobody knows whom against nobody knows
whom. Later (v. 3. 137), we hear of the King's "trusty
brother-in-law," whom, from the sarcastic tone, we
guess to be a traitor; but that is all the information
vouchsafed us; and with him is an abbot, also a traitor,
but not a hint is given that he is the very "lord of
Westminster" to whom, strangely enough, Carlisle, the
King's open enemy, had been committed for custody.
When (v. 6. 8) the heads of the conspirators are brought
to Henry, we are told that one of them is that of "Kent";
but it is not from Shakspere that we learn who Kent
is. Nor are these the only omissions; but they are
sufficient.

We open our Holinshed, and all (or nearly all) is
clear. The Duke of Surrey, being Richard's nephew, is
naturally opposed to Bolingbroke, and a main supporter
of Aumerle's conspiracy. In the early days of Henry's
reign, like Aumerle, he is deprived of his dukedom, and
thenceforward appears as *Earl of Kent*. Richard's half-
brother, the Duke of Exeter, is similarly reduced in
rank, and obliged to content himself with the Earldom
of Huntingdon. Exeter had married Henry's sister
Elizabeth, but in disgust at his degradation joined in
the conspiracy against his royal *brother-in-law*. As for
"the Abbot," we learn from Holinshed that the plot
against Henry was hatched *in a secret chamber of the
Abbot's house at Westminster*; where

by the advice of the Earle of Huntingdon, it was devised
that they should take upon them a solemn justes to be

enterprysed between him and twentie on his part, and the
erle of Salisburie and twentie with him, at Oxford, to the
which triumph king Henrie should be desired, and....
sodainly shoulde be slaine and destroyed.

All this was well known to Shakspere, who is following his authority with considerable closeness at this
point; but, *precisely because he himself knows it so well*,
he omits to give the requisite information to his hearers.

So far we had written, when we recollected that in
respect of one difficulty of a similar kind Johnson,
and even Pope, had been beforehand with us. Speaking
of the marked personal enmity of the Bastard Faulconbridge to the Duke of Austria, as repeatedly shown in
King John, Pope observes:

What was the ground of this quarrel is no where specify'd
in the present play; nor is there in this place (III. 1. 75 *sq.*),
or the scene where it is first hinted at (namely the second
of Act II) the least mention of any reason for it. But the
story is, that *Austria*, who killed *Richard Coeur-de-Lion*,
wore as the spoil of that Prince, a lion's hide which had
belong'd to him. This circumstance renders the anger of the
Bastard very natural and ought not to have been omitted[1].
In the first sketch of this play (which *Shakspere* is said to
have had a hand in, jointly with *William Rowley*) we accordingly find this insisted upon, and I have ventured to
place a few of these verses here.

Upon this Johnson comments as follows:

To the insertion of these lines I have nothing to object.
There are many other passages in the old play of great
value. The omission of this incident, in the second draught,
was natural. *Shakespeare, having familiarised the story to his*

[1] Pope might have added that it makes the death of Austria at the Bastard's hands
as striking a piece of poetic justice as the death of Macbeth at the hands of Macduff.

own imagination, forgot that it was obscure to his audience[1];
or, what is equally probable, the story was then so popular
that a hint was sufficient at that time to bring it to mind,
and these plays were written with very little care for the
approbation of posterity[2].

It is something to find oneself thus in harmony with
one of the sanest of Shaksperean critics. If we err,
it is a consolation to err with Plato.

---

[1] The italics are here mine.
[2] It is probably the influence of the old play—which in some respects has merits
not found in its successor—that accounts for those inconsistencies in the character
of the King which have puzzled commentators. To the old author John was a Protestant
champion, and his character is therefore consistently idealised. Shakspere, while
unable to omit this feature altogether, had other aspects of John in his mind: and these
at times, come into prominence to the detriment of psychological probability.

IV

Some Notes on a Feature of Shakspere's Style

THE Shakspere-criticism of Coleridge, like that of most of the Romantics, often strays into vague and unserviceable eulogy. His panegyric is sometimes so general that it loses all point. Thus, for example, when he contrasts Shakspere with Beaumont and Fletcher and with Massinger, by observing that "Shakspeare is universal, and, in fact, has no *manner*" (*Table Talk*, Feb. 17, 1833), he gives us as little real illumination as does Swinburne when indulging in a page or two of superlatives. But fortunately this is by no means always the case. Very often, especially when less eloquent than usual, he puts his finger on some really distinguishing characteristic of his hero; and it is precisely these unambitious passages that afford us the most help. It is, indeed, we believe, these touches of unostentatious insight, rather than the flights of general panegyric, which give to Coleridge his great and almost unique position as a critic. Thus (*Table Talk*, March 5, 1834) he remarks that

Shakspeare's intellectual action is wholly unlike that of Ben Jonson or Beaumont and Fletcher. The latter see the totality of a sentence or passage, and then project it entire. Shak-speare goes on creating, and evolving B out of A, and C out of B, and so on, just as a serpent moves, which makes a fulcrum of its own body, and seems for ever twisting and untwisting its own strength.

One might find flaws in the illustration, but the fact illustrated is beyond dispute, and it is emphatically worth notice. Coleridge had already hinted at it. On April 7, 1833, he tells us: "In Shakspeare one sentence begets the next naturally; the meaning is all inwoven. He goes on kindling like a meteor through the dark atmosphere."

The truth of these statements, within limits which we shall presently define, will be obvious to every attentive reader of the plays. It is, in fact, only another way of saying that Shakspere was a great dramatist. For a dramatist whose dialogue did not follow the twists and turns of apparent accident, and did not move by a kind of natural suggestion that artistically concealed art, and that mimicked with more or less success the dialogue of every-day life—such a writer would be no true dramatist at all. A scene in which the conversation proceeded as regularly as a proposition of Euclid, might possibly be admired, but it could never be heard through. And that the links between speech and speech, between thought and thought, if always present, are not always easily visible, is due to the fact that Shakspere was not only a dramatist but a lyric poet of the first rank, in whose writing emotion is a vital element. In his most passionate plays this emotion, though of course never escaping the law of association of ideas, constantly leaps from peak to peak like lightning in the Alps, and as completely forgets the laws of ordered "discourse" as does a Psalm of David. We thus find in Shakspere a phenomenon similar, amid a hundred dissimilarities, to a phenomenon constantly visible in the Epistles of St Paul: namely, that the thoughts do not follow a line previously traced out, but spring, extempore and by association, from a singularly fertile and ready mind.

To dwell on such a point as this may well seem to many a case of much ado about nothing. Every mind, it may be argued, is inevitably subject to the laws of association, and obeys them more or less obviously. Why insist on the fact that Shakspere's mind, though so stupendously comprehensive and alert, yet followed ordinary human law? We answer, first, that to trace the workings of *any* mind is, even at worst, a very interesting pastime; and secondly that in Shakspere, as we shall soon see, these ordinary laws worked in a very peculiar and extraordinary fashion, to such an extent indeed that our interest is doubled. Throughout his literary career, of course, his mind showed abnormal strength; but as his mental powers improved with practice, they developed a speed of movement which is almost a positive danger to the reader, who runs a constant risk of being deceived as our eyes are deceived by the skill of a prestidigitator. It is thus, unless we are willing to be so deceived, our duty to be constantly on the watch. If we think it desirable, as we surely do, to trace Shakspere's meaning as thoroughly as we can,

we must be *always* on guard, lest his amazing mental
speed should outstrip our too languid gaze.

One of the consequences of this characteristic in
Shakspere, on which it may be desirable to bestow a
word in passing, is that he, like Byron and other poets
of the rapid kind, depended on his first spring for
success. If he missed his prey, he retired growling to
his den. He was almost totally unable to *correct* either
his own writing or that of anyone else. He repeatedly
tried to do so; but no sooner had he begun the process
than the fury of creation seized him, and he re-wrote.
Thus it was with the great speech of Berowne in *Love's
Labour's Lost*; thus it was with many a passage in
Hamlet; thus, we may be sure, with *All's Well*. He
began by wishing merely to amend; he finished by
transforming. "Sentence begat sentence" so naturally
that he advanced like an impromptu orator who gathers
enthusiasm from the audience he is addressing. The
style of Shakspere, in this respect, is thus entirely different from the chastened and thoughtful style of such
a writer as Milton, in whose poems the sentence, however long, foresees its end, and prepares *deliberately* for
its successor.

Coleridge was thus indubitably right. But, though
right in the general scope of his assertion, he failed on
the one hand to limit it sufficiently, and on the other
to extend it far enough. He would have done better
had he discriminated between Shakspere's earlier plays
and his later; between the time when he was learning
his art and the time when he had mastered it; and,

equally, he ought to have pointed out the lengths to which, as Shakspere's rapidity of thought grew, this suggestive or associative method of composing carried him. Had he paused to consider the difference between earlier and later plays, he would have seen at once that this characteristic, though of course not invisible to a keen eye in the "apprentice" works, is by no means the most outstanding feature of their style. In the *Two Gentlemen of Verona*, for example, the manner is highly polished and elaborate—often, indeed, too much so for the content—but it shows little sign of the "evolution" of which Coleridge speaks. For a "tricksy word" it sometimes "defies the matter"; but it does not *advance* from that word. Many of these early plays have little *dramatic* merit, and therefore their dialogue and their sentence-construction fail, in this regard, to hold a true mirror up to nature. In real life, conversation does and must "evolve"; and so it does in Shakspere's later plays. But in his "apprentice-period" things are different. Even in *Romeo and Juliet* the dialogue is spasmodic: and this is one reason why *Romeo and Juliet*, while one of the greatest of dramatic *poems*, is hardly a great drama.

As we advance into the "Middle Period," however, we find this "evolution" growing more and more marked. Shakspere thinks as he writes; or rather, he does not need to pause for thought. Earlier, he struck out thoughts at intervals; later, his thoughts came too quickly for his hand to keep pace with them; but now, in his middle plays, thought and hand seem to move together. We can, indeed, almost watch him at the task of thinking, and see, as he would have expressed it, into "the quick forge and working-house of thought." Take, for one instance out of a hundred, the little speech of Orlando to his brother (*As You Like It*, I. I. 40): "Shall I keep your hogs and eat husks with them?"—instantly leading, by a process obvious and natural, to the next question, "What *prodigal* portion have I spent, that I should come to such penury?" Or the equally obvious traduction of Jaques's speech (II. 7. 43):

> Provided that you *weed* your better judgments
> Of all opinion that grows *rank* in them
> That I am wise.

Or take the almost too well-known oration of Henry V in answer to Westmorland—written, it may be re-membered, nearly contemporaneously with *As You Like It*. Throughout, but especially towards the end, the links of connection, though consisting less in merely verbal suggestions, are equally plain to the eye:

> We few, we happy few, we band of *brothers*:
> For he to-day that sheds his blood with me
> Shall be *my brother*; be he ne'er so vile,
> This day shall *gentle* his *condition*:
> And *gentlemen* in England now abed
> Shall think themselves accurst they were not here,
> And hold their *manhoods* cheap whiles any speaks
> That fought with us upon St Crispin's Day.

It was said of Burke that he wound himself into his subject like a serpent. Of Shakspere we may surely say that like a serpent he winds himself out of one subject into another. In the above passage we see how the word *brothers* in one line suggests *my brother* two lines below; how *gentle* leads on to *gentlemen*, and that to *manhoods*. This is not the slow and oft-pondered writing of a Virgil or a Tennyson; it is emphatically the extempore writing of a many times multiplied Scott or Dryden. To recur to our parallel with St Paul, there is a remarkable likeness amid differences between a style like this and the style of such a passage as the first chapter of the Epistle to the Ephesians, in which the Apostle's surging thoughts, far outpacing the pen of the panting Tertius, carry him at the end of a sentence to something that was certainly not in his mind at the beginning. In its reaching out to what is coming, and in its forgetfulness of what is past, a style like this reminds us of Time as described by Ulysses: it is "like a fashionable host, that slightly shakes his parting guest by the hand, and, with his arms outstretched as he would fly, grasps-in the comer." It is a *living* style, and speaks the vitality of the man who uses it.

But now let us go a little further, and take some passages from later plays. *Macbeth* is perhaps as good a specimen of the transition from the middle period to the latest as we are likely to find. In it, if there is not quite what Dowden calls that "perfect balance and equality between the thought and its expression" which is exhibited in *Julius Caesar* or *As You Like It*, there is not yet that "disturbance of the balance" which appears in the *Tempest* or in *Winter's Tale*. But we are on the way to that disturbance, and occasionally the language rather "hints or hesitates" the thought than expresses it. We have then to *guess* the suggestions on

which Shakspere's mind worked, for his speed is becoming too great for us to track it with certainty.

As illustrations, take first the Porter's speech—now
generally admitted to be genuine and characteristic of
Shakspere. The Porter, pretending to be at hell-gate,
says, "Here is a farmer, that hanged himself on an
expectation of plenty"—doubtless an allusion to some
farmer who actually had speculated on a bad harvest,
and then, seeing reason to fear a good one, committed
suicide. But then Shakspere's mind, turning on the
word "farmer," remembers half-unconsciously that
Garnet, the Jesuit who was hanged for supposed com-
plicity in the Gunpowder Plot, had been known by the
alias of "Mr Farmer." Hence the allusion to the
"equivocator who could not equivocate to heaven"
which comes two or three lines below: for, as is well
known, the "equivocations" of Garnet and his defence
of the general principle of equivocation had attracted
the attention of the whole country, and made Garnet's
name a proverb.

As we read further, we are struck at every turn by
the prevalence of the phenomenon in its various shapes
and aspects. Shakspere, in the scene of the discovery
of the murder, is working at a white heat, and his
imagination pictures the successive phases without
pause. Rapid, however, as is his thought, his writing
almost keeps pace with it, as if he were resolved that
none of his visions should be lost. We can perceive the
fiery speed with which the lines were jotted down: and
we are often permitted to see how one line gave birth

to the next. Sometimes—in a fashion which is more
fully exhibited in still later plays, and which we shall
illustrate more at length in a moment—it is a single
word on which his mind dwells for an instant, passing
in a flash from one association of the word to another.
Thus we hear of "dire combustion and confused events
new *hatched* to the woful time." What is that which
we naturally think of as being hatched? The next word
gives the answer: "The obscure *bird* clamoured the
livelong night": a mental process parallel to that of
Claudius in *Hamlet* (III. 1. 171):

> There's something in his soul
> O'er which his melancholy sits *on brood*;
> And I do doubt the *hatch and the disclose*
> Will be some danger.

A score of lines later we have another instance of the
same general class, but different in species: "From this
hour," says Macbeth, unconsciously prophesying,
"there's nothing serious in mortality; the *wine* of life
is drawn, and the mere lees is left this *vault* to brag
of": the body is thus suddenly compared to a vault in
which wine is kept, because the joy of life had just been
compared to wine itself. Again, the famous speech of
Macbeth, in which he overacts so fatally the attitude
of a loyal and innocent man, is nothing but one long
illustration of our point:

> Here lay Duncan,
> His *silver* skin laced with his *golden* blood;
> And his gashed stabs looked like a breach in nature
> For ruin's wasteful entrance: there, the murderers,
> Steeped in the colours of their trade, their daggers
> Unmannerly breeched with gore.

The excessively "conceited" character of this passage
is, of course, fully explained and justified by the nervous
irritability of the speaker's state at the moment: but it
should nevertheless be compared on the one hand with
the *deliberate* drawing-out of comparisons in which a
Richard II indulged in his prison, and on the other
hand with the swift, but yet light and easy, turn in the
speech of Metellus (*Julius Caesar*, II. 1. 143), urging the
inclusion of Cicero in the plot:

> O let us have him, for his *silver* hairs
> Will *purchase* us a good opinion.

It is safe to say that had *Macbeth* been written when
Richard II was written, the changes of metaphor
would have been less sudden; and that if it had been
written contemporaneously with *Julius Caesar*, the harsh
transitions would have been more smooth[1].

But *Macbeth* also marks the full manifestation of a
phenomenon which, while adumbrated in the earlier
plays, becomes a frequent and conspicuous feature of
the latest: namely, the advance made by means of a
paronomasia that is only suggested, and not fully expressed. An example may make what we mean clearer.
In the *Merchant of Venice* (III. 5. 83) Lorenzo tells
Jessica to reserve her witticisms for dinner: "then,"

---

[1] I am inclined however to think that this passage contains another punning
"suggestion," of a less smooth and obvious kind. "Our youths and wildness shall
no whit appear, but all be *buried* in his *gravity*." People are usually buried in graves,
and the grave suggests gravity at once. If we remember that *grave* was pronounced
grääv, this possibility will seem, I think, a probability. See Ellis, *Early English
Pronunciation*, p. 891, where he shows from Bullokar (A.D. 1580) that grave was so
pronounced; p. 991, for naked (= *nähked*), p. 62, for plague (= *plahg*), bake (= *bahk*),
etc. Falstaff's famous jest (*2 Henry IV*, I. 2. 184) makes our conjecture almost certain:
"There's not a white hair on your face," says the Chief Justice, "but should have his
effect of gravity." "His effect of gravy," replies the Knight.

says he, "howsoe'er thou speakest, 'mong other things
I shall *digest* it." Here the word *digest* involves a plain,
simple, and expressed pun. But in Perdita's speech
(*Winter's Tale*, IV. 3. 10):

> But that our feasts
> In every mess have folly, and the feeders
> *Digest* it with a custom,

the word *digest* does *not* precisely give us a pun. It
rather presents us with one of Shakspere's so-called
"mixed metaphors," in which, to put the case truly,
his mind has rushed so rapidly from one metaphor to
the other that *our* minds, like panting Time, toil after
him in vain. Nevertheless, it is closely allied to the
paronomasia, and is based upon it: and here we are
brought face to face with what to many has seemed the
most annoying and exasperating weakness in Shakspere's writing. Nothing, to the modern mind, is more
trite or less admirable than the pun: and certainly
nothing is to us less surprising than that puns are
possible. Yet to the Elizabethan mind it seems to have
come with the force of a new revelation as to the capacities of language, or like the discovery of Columbus
on the Western World. Men could not get over their
ever-new astonishment at observing that a word often
bears a double meaning, or that a sentence can be made
to signify the opposite of what it seems to say. The
contemporaries of Shakspere, and Shakspere himself,
revelled in this discovery as Ralegh and Gilbert
revelled in the chances of fortune that lay open to them
in some newly-found Virginia or El Dorado. "To see

this age!" says Feste in *Twelfth Night*, "A sentence is but a cheveril glove to a good wit: how quickly the wrong side may be turned outward!" Hence the quibbles in which Nicholas Bacon and his greater son so delighted; hence in part, perhaps, the very "equivocations" by which Garnet startled the world; hence in particular the eternal plays on words that crowd the dramas of the time. Shakspere, of course, is one of the prime exemplars of the fashion. Such a word as *light*, for instance, it is well known that he could never meet without punning on it. "What, must I hold a candle to my shames?" says Jessica in her boy's dress; "they of themselves, methinks, are too light." "Let me *give* light," says Portia, "but let me not *be* light; for a light wife doth make a heavy husband." The various meanings of *nothing*, again, supply endless chances of quibbling; and, as every reader of the *Sonnets* is aware, we have in these poems "*will* to boot, and *will* in *overplus*," often so entangled in its many significations that it is impossible to know which of them was uppermost in Shakspere's mind. To a man like Johnson, in whose view a pun was as bad as picking a pocket, all this was intensely repugnant; and the power of the quibble over Shakspere seemed like some malignant fascination, such as that exercised by a Cleopatra over an Antony, for which the poet thought the world of reason and propriety well lost. To us, on the other hand, it appears rather like the *naïveté* of youth. The same phenomenon is visible in all nations at certain stages in their history. It is no more visible in the Elizabethans than in the writers of Genesis; and it is a conspicuous feature in the so-called "irony" of Sophocles, in the wit of Aristophanes, and in the pathetic pessimism of Euripides. The grave Aeschylus himself does not disdain it. It is, then, not Shakspere that we must blame for its appearance, but his young and eager times. Even in Milton, as everybody is aware, the disease is not extinct, and twice or thrice in *Paradise Lost* itself, it is manifested with terrible results. But in Milton, as a rule, the same tendency of mind usually shows itself in nobler and more classical fashion, endeavouring to press out of a word, in one and the same sentence, all its English, Latin, or Greek *associations*, rather than to play upon its *meanings*.

As, then, Shakspere was inevitably subject to this influence, we shall constantly find his "intellectual action" taking its bent from it. His sentences will "evolve" themselves on the lines of a kind of paronomasia; and very often we shall see that his thought has taken a double edge because the word was double. He lights upon it in one of its senses, and before we have time to turn round we behold him leaving it in another. In his earlier plays he would have dwelt on the quibble, and perhaps even worried it to exhaustion; in his middle plays he makes full use of it, but generally does not overdo it; in his later, except for a special purpose, he just notices it, and, almost without regarding it, passes on. In *Love's Labour's Lost*, for instance, we have Moth and Costard endlessly punning on *odds*, *goose*, and the like. In *As You Like It* we find Jaques playing, twice in a page, on the word *suit*. "I am ambitious for a motley coat." "Thou shalt have one," says the Duke. "It is my only *suit*," says Jaques (II. 7. 43): and again (line 79):

> Or what is he of basest function,
> That says his *bravery* is not on my cost,
> Thinking that I mean him, but therein *suits*
> His folly to the mettle of my speech?

The same scene provides us with another example of this "middle period" manner. The Duke's mention of the "wide and universal *theatre*" suggests to Jaques his famous speech on the Seven Acts or Ages of men and women; a speech in which, as we might expect from the moralising habit of the speaker, the image is drawn out into "a thousand similes." But in *Macbeth*, written five or six years later, the process is much more rapid. "Ah, good father," says Ross (Act II. Sc. 4):

> Thou seest the heavens, as troubled with man's *act*,
> Threaten his bloody *stage*.

Here the word *act*, as it first occurred to the poet's mind, meant simply *deed*; but he has scarcely finished writing it down when it suggests to him the paraphernalia of the theatre.

Almost exactly parallel is the passage in a much later play (*Tempest*, Act II. Sc. 1):

> She that from whom
> We all were *sea-swallowed*, though some *cast* again,
> And by that destiny, to perform an *act*
> Whereof what's past is *prologue*, what to come
> In yours and my *discharge*.

We are not here concerned either with the grammar or with the reading of the passage; all that we wish to notice is that Antonio, in describing the adventures of the wedding-party after leaving Claribel in Tunis, proceeds by precisely the same "quibbling evolution," if we may so call it, as Ross in *Macbeth*. "In coming from Tunis," says he, "we were all swallowed up by the sea. Some, however, were cast up again." But the word *cast* at once suggests to his mind (or, rather to Shakspere's) the idea of casting for a play. Hence the successive phrases—*act* (with its own double sense), *prologue*, and *discharge* in its Shaksperean meaning of *performance*.

Very similar is the sudden leap in Prospero's account to Miranda (Act I. Sc. 2) of the conduct of his treacherous brother, who

Having both the *key*
Of officer and office, set all hearts in the state
To what tune pleased his ear.

As the thought of a key *entered* Prospero's mind, it was the idea simply of a key to unlock a door; but ere it *left*, it had become also the idea of a tuning-key: and the change is made so naturally and quickly that we scarcely notice it.

At times, indeed, it might have puzzled Shakspere himself to know on which of two possible meanings of a word his mental eye first fell. The effect is that of a "zeugma" in which the two ideas are practically co-existent. Take, as a typical instance, the lines that close the 69th Sonnet:

Then (churls) their thoughts, although their eyes were kind,
To thy fair flower add the rank smell of weeds;
But why thy odour matcheth not thy show,
The soil is this, that thou dost common grow.

Here it is impossible to tell whether the meaning of "proof, solution" which attaches to the word *soil*, or the more common meaning of soil in which flowers are planted, is the predominant one in the author's mind. One thing alone is certain, that neither by itself conveys the full sense of the passage. Similarly, when Perdita, in the *Winter's Tale* (IV. 3. 21), warns Florizel against the anger of his father:

> O the fates!
> How would he look, to see his work, so noble,
> Vilely bound up!—

it is difficult to say at what point exactly the conception of a "work" as a "volume" entered Shakspere's brain. It may have been simultaneously with its conception as a "child" or "son"; it may have been a moment later: but the transition, in any case, was made with amazing speed. Contrast it with the ordered deliberation of the passage describing Arthur in *King John* (II. 1. 103):

> Look here upon thy brother Geffrey's face:
> These eyes, these brows, were moulded out of his;
> This little abstract doth contain that large
> Which died in Geffrey, and the hand of time
> Shall draw this brief into as huge a volume.

It is safe to say that had these five lines been written in 1606 instead of a dozen years earlier, we should have seen the "large" five lines contracted into the "brief" of two or three pregnant words.

Similarly, when Antonio (*Tempest*, II. 1. 272) expresses the wish that twenty consciences, if they stood between him and his ambition, might be *candied* and *melt* ere they molested him, we can easily see that the idea of *sugaring over* came first, and the idea of *melting* second. But in the speech of the fallen Imperator (*Antony and Cleopatra*, IV. 10. 33):

> The hearts
> That spanieled me at heels, to whom I gave
> Their wishes, do discandy, melt their sweets,
> On blossoming Caesar; and this pine is barked
> That overtopped them all:

who can keep up with the rapidity of Shakspere's light fantastic turns of thought? We can see how *discandy* combines both conceptions, that of *sweet* and that of *melting*; we can discern how *spanieled* suggested *barked*[1], and how that led to *pine* and to *blossom*; but the speed of the transitions is beyond us, and the intermediate stages are often for ever lost.

At times, as we have seen, this mental habit of Shakspere leads him into ineffable futilities; at times it carries him to supernatural heights. What could be worse than this? (*Henry V*, II. Chorus, 25):

> Three corrupted men
> Have for the *gilt* of France, O *guilt* indeed,
> Confirmed conspiracy with fearful France.

What, on the other hand, could be better than Lady Macbeth's similar play on the same words? (*Macbeth*, II. 2. 56)[2]:

> I'll *gild* the faces of the grooms withal,
> For it must seem their *guilt*.

---

[1] *King Lear*, III. 6. 60:

> The little dogs and all,
> Tray, Blanch, and Sweetheart, see they bark at me.

[2] Danton's tremendous pun just before his execution is the nearest parallel in history that occurs to us.

But the futility and the splendour spring from exactly the same cause, and it is in a sense an accident when the effect is great. It is certain that Shakspere would not have resisted the quibble even if its effect had been to spoil the force of the scene. Fortunately, his mind was generally so attuned to the prevailing tone of his scenes, that he rarely struck upon a quibble that *did* ruin their force.

It is worth notice that in *Hamlet*—perhaps the most rapid in thought, as it is the slowest in action, of all Shakspere's plays—the peculiar kind of verbal evolution on which we are here dwelling is rarely found. We have indeed a marked example of it in the speech of Laertes to Ophelia (I. 3. 12)—

> As this *temple* waxes,
> The inward *service* of the mind and soul
> Grows wide withal:

in which the double use of *service* is obvious, derived as it is from the employment of the word *temple* for the human body. But the general style of *Hamlet* is better illustrated by the later speech of Polonius in the same scene:

> Do not believe his vows, for they are brokers,
> Not of that dye which their investments show,
> But mere implorators of unholy suits,
> Breathing like sanctified and pious bawds,
> The better to beguile:

in which, though the presence of the paronomasia-motive is not to be denied, the main feature is rather an extraordinary rapidity in change of metaphor, suggested rather by contiguity in *thought* than by the mere wealth of a *word*. So far, indeed, as it is lawful to distinguish between an idea and its expression, we may perhaps say that in *Hamlet* the rapidity is due more to the intense sympathy with which Shakspere realises the changes in his hero's *mind*, especially as the situation in which he is placed alters, than to an evolution in the words themselves. The situation begets a state of mind, and that state of mind, being remarkably complex and unstable, begets in its turn a remarkably entangled and even confused method of expressing itself[1].

And now, by the light of the passages we have just been noticing, let us consider one that has attracted the puzzled interest of commentators and ordinary readers for many generations—Cassio's famous panegyric on Desdemona (*Othello*, II. 1. 60). In answer to Montano's question, "Is your general wived?" Cassio replies:

> Most fortunately: he hath achieved a maid
> That paragons description and wild fame;
> One that excels the quirks of blazoning pens,
> And in the essential vesture of creation
> Does tire the ingener.

Here there has been much difference as to the correct reading. The Quartos, for "tire the ingener," have

[1] It is of course unnecessary to remark that the above statements apply solely to the *style* of *Hamlet* the play. Nothing is more obvious than the fact that the sayings of the Prince, throughout the play, and especially those cryptic utterances which he uses when acting the madman, are full of examples of this associative law. Two specimens out of a hundred will suffice. The oath by St Patrick (I. 5. 136) seems to be suggested by the serpent that "stung" the King; and it is quite possible, as Dowden hints, that Hamlet's words "Let not the soul of Nero enter this firm bosom" (III. 2. 360) arise from a sub-conscious memory that Agrippina, the mother of Nero, was the wife of Claudius. But all these are revelations rather of the mind of Hamlet than of the style of Shakspere.

"bear all excellency," a version accepted by Rowe and
Pope; but justly termed by Steevens "flat and un-
poetical." Most editors, indeed, since Johnson have
seen in it either Shakspere's first thoughts, or the mere
blunder of some piratical copyist. The four Folios, with
but the usual varieties of spelling, give "Tire the In-
geniver," for which all sorts of alterations have been
suggested, from the possible "tire the ingenious verse"
or "tire the inventor" down to the ludicrous "tire the
Indian ever."

If, as is surely legitimate, we reject the Quarto
reading as at least not Shakspere's final correction, it
will at once dawn on our readers that we desire to
retain the word *tire*, and that all substitutes, such for
example as *try*, ought in our opinion to be refused. For
tire has the Shaksperean mark of being suggested by the
preceding phrase "essential vesture." From that, his
mind naturally darted to *attire* or *tire*. The process was
the same as, but much more rapid than, that by which
(to add one more example to the many already adduced)
Constance in *King John* (III. 4. 101) passes from *form*
(*i.e.* head-gear) in one line to *disorder* (deformity) in
the next:

> I will not keep this form upon my head,
> When there is such disorder in my wit.

But, even before the word *tire*, in this sense (familiar
to all of us ever since we first read that Jezebel "painted
her face and *tired* her head"), had been written down,
Shakspere's mind had hurried to its other meaning of
weary, exhaust: and it is this latter meaning, of course,

that predominates in the passage almost to the entire
exclusion of the other. We can figure the process to ourselves as follows: "Desdemona surpasses all description and the wildest exaggerations of report: Nature,
when she attired her in that lovely vesture, made her
out-tire all other women, and achieved such perfection
that it *tires* the highest powers of invention to describe
her." The same idea is put, less compactly and less
intricately, in two other passages of Shakspere. Miranda,
according to Prospero, "outstrips all praise and makes
it halt behind her"; and Portia, in the view of Bassanio,
excelled the creative power of the "demigod" who had
painted her portrait. In neither of these passages, however, is there anything like the same suddenness of
thought-transition as we see here.

But we have not yet exhausted Cassio's meaning;
for, as a little thought will show, the word *ingener* is
also of double significance. Not only does it connote
an inventive and imaginative *describer*—in which sense
it carries on the idea of the "blazoning pens"; but it
also conveys the suggestion of a *maker*—in which sense
it refers us back to "creation." The beauty of Desdemona
not only is too high for description, but—in the enthusiastic hyperbole of Cassio—actually wearied its very
creator, who needed a rest after finishing his work. We
remember how, in the hundred and fourth Psalm, God
is said to clothe the earth with light "sicut *vestimento*";
and how, in the second chapter of Genesis, he rested
from his toil.

We could easily bring forward scores of other instances

more or less similar in kind to these; but perhaps the reader has had sufficient. If any should be inclined, like Johnson, to regard these playings with words as indicating that Shakspere, after all, was for an age and not for all time, we might incidentally remind them that he shares this characteristic with many another great man. Paul himself, in writing to a friend, did not disdain to point a petition with a light play on a name; and one of the sublimest poets that ever lived, who wrote in a far distant period from Shakspere's and in a very different language, had the same peculiarity. Isaiah, seven hundred years before Christ, had the Shaksperean love of a paronomasia; nay, on one occasion he uses it to add force to the tremendous close of a lofty denunciation: "He looked for judgment, and behold oppression; for righteousness, and behold a cry"— he looked for *mishpat*, and behold *mispach*; for *tsedakah*, and behold *tse'akah*. Of such companionship even Shakspere might be proud; and in such surroundings the humble pun is raised to an almost royal dignity. He, in fact, who despiseth it despiseth life itself.

V

Shakspere's Children

NEXT to thoughtless blame, nothing is easier to a critic than indiscriminate praise; and nothing is more useless. It is a pleasure to think that such praise is now ceasing to be showered upon Shakspere, and that we are being at last allowed both to admire and to censure with a certain measure of discretion. "Nothing to extenuate, and to set down naught in malice "—this should be our motto; our duty towards Shakspere should be to speak of him as Brutus spoke of Caesar, neither diminishing his glory wherein he was worthy, nor enforcing his offences, which at their worst cannot dim his fame.

Nowhere has Shakspere suffered more of this uncritical eulogy than in reference to his children. Swinburne, for example, deals always in superlatives; but his superlatives are never more shrill or inarticulate than when he speaks of Shakspere's "heavenly family" of little boys. On Mamillius he lavishes all his flowers. Of Arthur this is what he says:

I am not minded to say much of Shakespeare's Arthur; there are one or two figures in the world of his work of which there are no words that would be fit or good to say. The place they have in our lives and thoughts is not one for talk; the niche set apart for them to inhabit in our secret hearts is not penetrable by the lights and noises of common day. There are chapels in the cathedral of man's highest art as in that of his inmost life, not made to be set open to

the eyes and feet of the world. Love and death and memory
keep charge for us in silence of some beloved names. It is
the crowning glory of genius, the final miracle and transcen-
dant gift of poetry, that it can add to the number of these,
and engrave on the very heart of our remembrance fresh
names and memories of its own creation.

So much for Swinburne on "this bud of Britain,"
"this most famous flower in a princely trinity of boys"
—and so on, with his usual profusion of adjectives.
But other critics, less exuberant than Swinburne as a
rule, are on this point not less eloquent than he. One
can find traces of this eloquence in the fragmentary
notes that alone remain of Coleridge's lectures; and it
is constantly blazing forth in the pages of Brandes.
Such a consensus of opinion may well make us more
than usually doubtful of the truth of our own opinion;
to censure Shakspere at all is daring enough, but to
censure him where so many have praised him is the
height of presumption. And yet, after all our hesitations,
the truth has to be told. We do not like Shakspere's
children, nor can any effort make us like them.

It mitigates our sense of over-audacity a little to
remember that, as far as we can judge, Shakspere with
all his genius and all his observation had less chance
of knowing children than very ordinary people have to-
day. For he lived in times when children grew old fast
—and, indeed, had to grow old fast in self-defence; for
the barriers between the child and the adult were rigid,
and the child was kept in his place by the severest of
disciplines. When children were to be seen and not
heard, the chances of studying the inner mind of child-

hood were slight indeed. Even now, it is painfully
difficult for a grown-up person to enter that sanctuary;
what must it have been then? Few grown-up persons,
indeed, seem to have even wished to enter it. Hence,
as the *child* was suppressed, the only chance for him
was to imitate his elders, and to emerge as quickly as
possible into the more advanced stage. Thus—and not
merely because of her Southern blood—Juliet is a
woman at fourteen; Wolsey—not merely because the
University was then more of a school than now—is a
Bachelor of Arts at fifteen; Henry VIII rules a kingdom
at eighteen. A Lady Jane Grey had, indeed, scarcely
a childhood at all. No wonder that, when this whole
part of life was thus cut out, a John of Gaunt at fifty-
eight seems to Shakspere a tottering old man.

Thus, partly because Shakspere did not and could not
know children well, and partly because those he did
know were of this precocious kind, the children in his
plays are not child-like at all. He had doubtless been
a clever child himself. His own son, as became the
offspring of such a father, may well have been cleverer
than most. But whatever the explanation, we notice in
all these children the unfailing symptoms of the thorough
prig. They are all forward and pedantic; all are of the
class stigmatised by Gilbert as "children who are up
in dates," and who "never will be missed." Every one
of them, like little William in the *Merry Wives of
Windsor*, might have been described by Sir Hugh Evans
as "a good sprag memory"; and Mrs Page might say
of each of them, "He is a better scholar than I thought

he was." Moth, for example, the earliest of the breed,
is a *concettisto* who out-Armadoes Armado himself, and
who puns on everything punnable with a skill which
would have made Dr Johnson look to his pockets. By
his "penny of observation," as he tells his master, he
has purchased an experience which would not disgrace
a man of forty; and he can balance sentences as well
as Lyly himself. It might perhaps be objected that
Moth is an unfair example; he is "conceited" indeed,
but the whole play is one long conceit, and his twists
and turns belong rather to his creator than to himself.
This is true enough; but be it observed that in this play
of prigs a child is the most priggish, and that in a play
which is all Euphuism a child is the most euphuistic.
Still, even if we pass over *Love's Labour's Lost* as a
youthful extravagance, how fares it as we go farther
down the stream? What of *Richard III*, a play immature indeed, but pointing towards maturity? Here
we have two pairs of children, the "brats of Clarence"
and the two ill-fated princes. The Clarences are the less
objectionable—probably because we see very little of
them: but that little is enough to indicate that they are
of the same breed as the rest; their questions reveal a
precocious wisdom which is of a piece with the precocity
of all Shakspere's children. As for the little princes,
their forwardness is a portent. To quote the enthusiastic
words of Brandes, "the oldest child already shows
greatness of soul, a kingly spirit, with a deep feeling for
the import of historic achievement. The younger brother
is childishly witty, imaginative, full of boyish mockery

for his uncle's grimness, and eager to play with his dagger and sword." In other words, they are senti- mental, pert, and over-clever for their age; while York adds to these qualities those of an *enfant terrible* in rich measure; he is, in his mother's words, "too shrewd, a parlous boy." His puns are perhaps rather Shakspere's than his own: Gloucester tells him that the sword is too heavy for him to wear—

> *York.* I weigh it lightly, were it heavier.
> *Gloucester.* What, would you have my weapon, little lord?
> *York.* I would, that I might thank you as you call me.
> *Gloucester.* How?
> *York.* Little.

These are quibbles which we find in Jessica and in Parolles; hence perhaps we must not blame little York too much for them. But once again it is to be noticed that Shakspere, when inclined to quibbling and playing with words, seems to fancy that children are the most natural of his characters to whom to assign his quibbles. As for the young Prince Edward, his forwardness takes a different character; he has actually learnt to sift testi- mony like a historian, and wishes to know whether a reported feat of Julius Caesar is duly authenticated, or merely traditional. Such boys may be found in life, but are not common; our point is that *all* Shakspere's boys are of this kind, and that he seems to have known no other.

Of them all, however, Arthur is the worst. Literature, for some reason or other, has always more or less shunned the prig, or at least has usually been milder to

him than he deserves. Every other type of character has
been occasionally exaggerated by novelists or dramatists;
the villain is more villanous, the hero more heroic, in
literature than in life. But the prig of books is assuredly
less priggish than he of actuality. For this reason we
cannot say that we have not met, walking about in the
work-a-day world, worse prigs than even Arthur. But
this we *can* say, that of all prigs we ever read of in
books, Harry Sandford and the schoolboys in *Eric* not
excepted, Arthur is the most undiluted and the most
consummate. And Shakspere has gone out of his way
to make him so; for it is obvious that the boy is meant
to be several years younger than the fourteen or fifteen
years of the historical character whose name he has
taken. Sorrow has often made children prematurely
old: it is well known, for example, that the little
Louis XVII showed a strange knowledge of things
beyond the usual capacity of a boy of nine. But no
child, however unhappy, ever dealt in such repartees as
those of Arthur to Hubert, or was ever quite so epi-
grammatic in his language:

> Hubert, the utterance of a brace of tongues
> Must needs want pleading for a pair of eyes.

This is the antithetical style of a Johnson writing one
of his *Ramblers*: no boyish boy ever thus spoke, or ever
will thus speak, when really and deeply moved. Still
less will he play with trivialities like these:

> There is no malice in this burning coal:
> The breath of heaven hath blown his spirit out,
> And strewed repentant ashes on his head.

When Hubert replies that he can revive it with his breath, this astonishing child rejoins:

> An if you do, you will but make it blush
> And glow with shame of your proceedings, Hubert:
> Nay, it perchance will sparkle in your eyes,
> And, like a dog that is compelled to fight,
> Snatch at his master that doth tarre him on.
> All things that you should use to do me wrong
> Deny their office: only you do lack
> The mercy that fierce fire and iron extends,
> Creatures of note for mercy-lacking uses.

These are the conceits of a Belial on the plains of heaven, or of a Richard II when he gives his fancy full play; but they are not the pleadings of a boy truly frightened about his eyes. Even in Richard, the image of a fire mourning in ashes for a deposed king is a little too far-fetched; in Arthur it is beyond measure absurd. No acting, be it that of Kate Terry herself, can make this talk sound natural; and, in fact, as a rule this scene, like the "sportful malice" of Sir Toby against Malvolio, "rather plucks on laughter than revenge"; it is recognised at once as artificiality of the most mechanical kind. It is safe to say that, when it succeeds, its success is due to the actor's suppression of the actual words, and reliance upon gestures and tears to draw the attention of the audience from the frigidity of their imagery— an imagery more worthy of Cowley's *Mistress* than of an impassioned child. Yet Brandes can actually think this scene drawn from some real scene between Shakspere and his son Hamnet! If so, then Hamnet must have been the most hide-bound and unnatural of little boys.

There is, with but slight and superficial differences, the same character repeated in the young Macduff and in Mamillius—a sameness astonishing in the myriad-minded Shakspere, and seeming to show that in very truth his acquaintances among boys were exceedingly few. Both Macduff and Mamillius, like young York, are pert as well as shrewd and over-sharp. If anyone thinks this judgment too harsh, let him get the un-biassed opinion of a dozen English schoolboys upon these little fellows. It will be unanimous, and it will be uncompromising. It is probable that any reputation less securely anchored than that of Shakspere would have foundered on a scene like that between little Macduff and his mother; but such is the force of pre-scription that we are bidden to admire it, and most of us imagine that we *do* admire it. But let the reader fancy to himself that a mere Middleton wrote it, and then ask himself what in very truth he thinks of it:

Lady Macduff.   Sirrah, your father's dead:
And what will you do now? How will you live?
    Son. As birds do, mother.
    L. Macd. What, with worms and flies?
    Son. With what I get, I mean; and so do they.
    L. Macd. Poor bird! thou'dst never fear the net, nor lime,
The pitfall, nor the gin.
    Son. Why should I, mother? *Poor birds they are not set for.*
My father is not dead, for all your saying.
    L. Macd. Yes, he is dead: how wilt thou do for a father?
    Son. Nay, how will you do for a husband?
    L. Macd. Why, I can buy me twenty at any market.
    Son. Then you'll buy 'em to sell again.
    L. Macd. Thou speak'st with all thy wit,
And yet, i' faith, with wit enough for thee.

Son. Was my father a traitor, mother?
L. Macd. Ay, that he was.
Son. What is a traitor?
L. Macd. Why, one that swears and lies.
Son. And be all traitors that do so?
L. Macd. Every one that does so is a traitor, and must be hanged.
Son. Who must hang them?
L. Macd. Why, the honest men.
Son. Then the liars and swearers are fools, for there are liars and swearers enough to beat the honest men, and hang up them.
L. Macd. Now God help thee, poor monkey! But how wilt thou do for a father?
Son. If he were dead, you'd weep for him: if you would not, it were a good sign I should quickly have a new father.

Let anyone pay impartial attention to the speeches italicised in this passage, and let him then honestly say whether, if they were less familiar, they would not seem worthier of a Benedick or a Beatrice in a "flyting-match" than of a simple little boy. It may be answered that this particular boy is not simple. Precisely so; he is sophisticated, and *so is every other of Shakspere's boys.* Our point is just this, that Shakspere has given us no variations on the type boy. Yet, in nature, boys are as various as men; and had Shakspere known them as he knew men, he would have varied them as he varied his statesmen, his soldiers, and his kings. But as a matter of fact his boys are as like each other as Charles Reade's women.

Mamillius, for example, only differs from young Macduff in the degree, but not in the kind, of his precocious pertness. He has learnt as much philosophy

out of women's faces as Berowne learnt from women's
eyes; he can generalise from the experience of his few
seasons, and declare that a sad tale is best for winter;
and amid the impertinences of his little lecture to the
waiting-ladies he contrives to show off a good deal of
mature observation. It may be that Hermione is fore-
boding a coming trouble, or it may be that she is fretted
by the departure of Polixenes; but in any case it is
notable that she finds the boy so troublesome that " 'tis
past enduring." Even the tale, which to Swinburne's
sorrow was never finished, of the man who dwelt by
a churchyard, is introduced by a cynical and adult-like
gibe at "yond crickets" the women. Still less like a
boy is the manner of his death, which indeed is the
most precocious disease in literature. He had a right
to die; but no child, of anything like the age apparently
assigned to Mamillius, ought to die for such a reason.

There is, in fact, but one boy in all Shakspere who
even appears to promise some genuine variation from
this perverse type. Young Coriolanus, in the line and
a half allotted to him,

A shall not tread on me;
I'll run away till I'm bigger, but then I'll fight,

utters the solitary truly boy-like sentiment in the whole
of Shakspere's plays. Alas! like Marcellus, he is but
shown and then withdrawn; he is only once put in
person before us, and he seems to be rather an allegorical shadow of his father than an independent living
being. We pass over here the boy in *Henry V* and the
fool in *King Lear*, both of whom, though seemingly very

young, are beyond the age of childhood. Even in them, however, there are traces, visible to those who care to look, that their infancy, so recently left behind, was of a thoroughly Shaksperean character. We could wish that Shakspere had not made it seem as if this character was typical and representative of the genus boy: and we may be sure that he would have given us many very different child-types if he had felt something of that interest in children which Dickens, for example, possessed. But to expect this from an Elizabethan is to expect the impossible; even Shakspere could not rise altogether above his age.

It is, in fact, only the astonishing breadth of Shakspere's treatment of older people that makes us notice the narrowness that marks his treatment of children. No one remarks on the same narrowness in Milton or in Ben Jonson. But Shakspere is so great that we ask more from him than in the nature of things he could give. And yet nothing but harm can be done by failing to state the exact truth. As child-psychology is a modern science, so Shakspere's knowledge of children contrasts very unfavourably with that of relatively far inferior writers of the last fifty years. His children are colourless beside Charlotte Bronte's, or Stevenson's, or even George MacDonald's, and are drawn with vastly less penetration. Nor again, to test him on the poetical side as distinct from the dramatic, does he show the slightest vestige of the Wordsworthian view of the child as a prophet or blest seer. All this, of course, proves no inferiority in him to Wordsworth—still less, of course, his inferiority to the crowd of other writers. But it *does* show the immense advance our age has made as compared with the Elizabethan in at least this one respect—sympathy with children and an eagerness to understand them. When the greatest of the Elizabethans can give us no better studies of children than those we have just considered, then we can congratulate ourselves that the progress of knowledge and of feeling has drawn children into its net, and made us resolve to understand and to realise them. The old idea of forcing them into our mould is, we trust, dead for ever. We recognise, as Spinoza did with reference to mankind in general, that our duty to them is *neque lugere, neque ridere, sed intelligere*; and, further, to look on them *sub specie aeternitatis*.

VI

Shakspere and Marriage

To judge a dramatist or a novelist by the opinions expressed by his puppets is a mistake in any case. Few would imagine, for instance, that Thackeray would have defended all that is said by Barnes Newcome, or that Dickens would have endorsed all the views of Quilp: nor must we draw conclusions as to the ideas of the author of Job from those of Elihu the son of Barachel. Still greater would be such a blunder in the case of Shakspere. Others, when the question is put to them with a certain amount of vigour, "abide" it: but he, who is all men at one time or another, remains "free." What Shakspere did, we know; what he was, in spite of all the psychological analysis of writers like Brandes, remains as obscure as ever.

Yet we must not press this sound principle too far. There is much that we can tell about the intellectual and moral character of Shakspere, and this without identifying him with Prospero or with Jaques. To judge him by the words of his creations would lead us astray; but the general conduct of his plots, the atmosphere of his plays, is an infallible guide to his opinions within a certain range. For instance, we can gather from *Henry IV*, in conjunction with the sister-dramas, that Shakspere was a firm believer in Nemesis, and saw that crime, however apparently successful, is punished at the

last. From *King John* or from *Richard II* we see
Shakspere's strong faith in the destiny of England as
clearly as if he had, after the fashion of Aristophanes,
silenced Faulconbridge or Gaunt for a moment in order
to declare his own views in a parabasis. We shall run
no great risk if we assert, on the sole evidence of the
plays, that Shakspere, whether he despised mobs or not,
believed in a monarchy; that he was firmly, if not
violently, opposed to the Puritans; that, in literary
matters, he belonged to the romantic rather than to the
classical school; and that he had a strong bias towards
supernaturalism and fatalism.

More difficult perhaps to arrive at, but more infallibly
certain when gained, is a conception of Shakspere's
character and circumstances from his works. Even apart
from the revelations of the *Sonnets* it would, we fancy,
be possible to gather that he was a man of very strong
passions, which he was at times utterly unable to control. It is clear, from the plays alone, that for several
years he was the victim of a terrible depression,
leading to the gloomiest views of life; so much so, in
fact, that when he set out to write a comedy he produced in *Measure for Measure* perhaps the most sombre
of all his works. It is equally clear that he to some extent escaped from this imprisonment—yet so as by fire.

But there is one subject on which unquestionably, as
can be shown from the plays, he held certain opinions:
opinions which inevitably reacted upon the very construction of his dramas, and which, in our view, not
only betoken a serious defect in his personal character,

but also are the source of some of the worst and most glaring faults in his literary work. This subject is that of marriage. It has been customary to gloss over these views of Shakspere as if they mattered little. Even Harris, the whole object of whose volume is to discover the man Shakspere behind the books, scarcely touches on this point at all[1]. Yet, whatever excuse we may find, it is certain that Shakspere held these views: certain, *not* because he puts them into the mouth of any particular *dramatis persona*, but because his plays could not have been as they are unless he had held these opinions. These ideas may or may not have been the ideas of his age or of his set also; in any case they were his own, and they were low and demoralising. It is useless to slur them over, as the critics do; it is equally useless to maintain that they are literary or conventional views, not carried out in practice; for they are of a kind, and are betrayed in a way, that would have been impossible if they had not been part and parcel of their owner; if, in fact, he had not held them so long that he had almost ceased to be conscious of anything abnormal or personal in them. Over and over again a marriage is the means used to solve a difficulty in a plot; and over and over again the marriage is of such a kind that no gentleman would, even in imagination, have had recourse to it to solve any difficulty whatever. In the following pages we shall endeavour to show that on this question Shakspere held views so degrading that it is impossible to

[1] There has been a considerable change in the attitude of critics in the last few years, yet it is plain that many of them are still afraid to say out what they think.

regard him as a man of lofty or strict character; while, on the other hand, we shall endeavour to show that these views were in a way their own punishment, inasmuch as they constitute by far the most serious *literary* defect in Shakspere's work.

Let us take first the view of marriage illustrated in the *Two Gentlemen of Verona*, a play indeed belonging, in all probability, to Shakspere's prentice period, but —like several of his early works—showing a finished execution which is often absent in the more rapidly-written later plays. It is true that, as so often, the con-cluding Act is huddled up and hasty; but it may be taken as certain that the extraordinary use of marriage here made is not due to mere carelessness.

Proteus, a young fellow who is described on the title page as a "gentleman," and whose friend Valentine regards him as complete with all the graces, is really more truly to be denominated an almost unmitigated cad; indeed his servant Launce does not mince the matter, and calls him plainly a knave. He loves, and is loved by, a young woman named Julia; but no sooner does he cast his eyes on Silvia, the fiancée of his friend Valentine, than he throws to the winds all thought of Julia, slanders and betrays Valentine, and finally, in the most brutal manner, attempts the honour of Silvia. Ere long Valentine discovers the dastardly treachery of his friend, whom fortune puts into his power. What happens? Two courses only are open to Valentine, who is plainly represented as no cur. He may give Proteus the horse-whipping he so richly deserves; this is the sort of action to be expected from a man of honour, and the sort which the meekest would not condemn. Or, on the other hand, he may act as a Christian, and forgive Proteus, recognising that the rarer action is in virtue than in vengeance; but he will, we are sure, protect Silvia at all hazards from the brutal wretch who has insulted her. Nothing else, we can safely assert, is possible: and Valentine does neither! A few words of penitence from Proteus are sufficient to disarm his wrath; and then this "gentleman," regardless entirely of Silvia's outraged feelings, sacrifices his love to his friendship, and hands over the "holy and pure" girl to be married by the libertine! The situation is indeed saved by the timely appearance of Julia, the first of the long list of Shakspere's Amazon heroines, who accomplishes an even greater miracle than Portia herself. At the sight of her Proteus performs a still more impossible repentance than at first; Julia forgives him as easily as he had forgotten her; and all, in accordance with Shakspere's easy philosophy of life, comes right in the end. There are many sudden and worthless repentances in the plays; over and over again it would seem that a man who has committed the worst of offences has only to confess in order to make all straight; but it is safe to say that no more shameful view of marriage was ever exhibited to the world than is shown here, alike in the Gordian knot of the play and in the device for its unravelling. And the crime is the more inexcusable as Shakspere, even when he wrote the *Two Gentlemen of Verona*, had no low view of woman-

kind as such. One might pardon a man who held woman
as a mere toy; but that a poet, after drawing, even in
outline, such a Silvia as this, should subject her to such
a fate, is surely one of the most extraordinary examples
of inconsistency ever seen. Much of course has been
written of the Renaissance view of marriage and of its
supposed inferiority to friendship. We are not ignorant
of Michael Angelo's extravagant expressions of devotion
to Tommaso Cavalieri, or of Philip Sidney's declaration
to Languet—"The chief enjoyment of my life, next to
the everlasting blessedness of heaven, will always be the
enjoyment of true friendship; and there you shall have
the chiefest place"—or of the hundred other proofs
that can be given that the knights of that age, *sans peur
et sans reproche*, held views of women very different
from those held by the knights of previous centuries.
A similar problem, and a similar solution, are presented
in the *Sonnets*, where, indeed, if Shakspere be the
protagonist, he plays a part as sorry as that of Valentine
himself; nay, perhaps, a worse; for he tells *his* Proteus,
who has behaved fully as badly as the Veronese gentleman, to take not one of his loves only, but all. But,
Renaissance or no Renaissance, anyone who could treat
even an imaginary Silvia—holy, fair, and wise, commended of all the swains—or in fact the Dark Lady
herself with all her faults, in such a manner as this,
deserves little credit for delicacy of feeling. Nor, we
may add, could a man who represents Silvia as ac-
quiescing, even by silence, have *understood* a good
woman however well he might *represent* her. It is no

defence that Proteus is put before us as a knave, and, as we have seen, is proclaimed as such by Launce. The point is not the knavery of Proteus, but the grovelling baseness of Valentine, and the want of consciousness *in the dramatist* that Silvia is degraded by such treatment. The idea seems to be that a woman is no more to a man than a principality to diplomatists; that she may be insulted as much as he pleases, and that at the close of a period of brutal violence all will be set right by an annexation in which she has no voice. After being grievously injured, in fact, she is to find full compensation in sharing the name of her injurer. How different is Shakspere's treatment of all this from Chaucer's direct censure of the Marquis Walter's behaviour to Grisilde!

> Though som men preise it for a subtil wit,
> But as for me, I seye that yuel it sit
> Tassaye a wyf whan that it is no nede,
> And putten her in anguish and in drede.

It may be argued that the *Two Gentlemen* is an early and immature play, and that we must not judge the Shakspere of forty by the Shakspere of twenty-seven. Early the play probably is. Let us then take a mature one, and see whether the dramatist had reformed in the interval. We might do worse than select *Much Ado about Nothing*, a comedy universally dated about 1599. Behind lay the *Merchant of Venice, Henry IV* and *Henry V*; the man who had written these was certainly mature. How then does he deal with marriage in this play? Claudio, a young gentleman of about the same

social position as Proteus, hears, on authority which he
ought to have suspected, that Hero, the lady he is to
marry, is not all that she should be. Not staying to
investigate the charge, not even mentioning to Hero's
father that he had any suspicions, this precious fellow
allows all the preparations for the marriage to go on
as before, and even permits the actual ceremony to
begin; when, with a brutality worthy of Proteus himself, he repudiates the girl publicly with every mark of
contumely and scorn. Hero faints, and indeed all but
dies, under the shock of this sudden cruelty, which
would indeed have been beyond measure brutal if she
had been as guilty as she was really innocent. It is not
long, however, before thoroughly Shaksperean justice is
done. Hero's innocence is established; Claudio repents;
and, thinking Hero actually dead, volunteers to marry
anyone whom Leonato, her injured father, may choose
for him. Leonato takes the opportunity of restoring
Hero to him at the new marriage-ceremony. Hero, for
all that appears, freely forgives him. "Mary pity
women"; what times were those, when an insult so
brutal could be supposed atoned for by so brutal a con-
cession! Hero forgives Claudio because Claudio within
a day or two after her supposed death is willing to marry
someone else! It is hard to prove a universal negative;
but we venture to say that no woman, from Eve down-
ward, ever has forgiven, or can be expected to forgive,
an injury so great as Claudio's apology. But what shall
we say of Leonato? He knows Claudio to be at the
very best a man prone to believe evil on the slightest

provocation or none; yet, without compunction, he hands over his daughter to this poor creature's protection for the rest of her natural life. The author, with all the chances that the dramatic art allows him, expresses no disapproval, and calmly entitles his play *Much Ado about Nothing*; as if the surprise were not rather that so little ado is made over so great a scoundrelism as that of Claudio! Here again the underlying implication is obvious. Man is so superior a being that if he condescends to offer a woman the slightest apology for a wrong he has done to her, she must accept it as the condescension of a god, take all his confessions as works of supererogation, and finally imagine the crime her own and apologise herself. All this is so rooted in Shakspere's mind that it scarcely seems to require assertion; it is assumed as a law of nature. It reminds one of Boswell's *naïve* remark to Mrs Knowles, who expressed a hope that in the next world the sexes will be equal: "That is too ambitious, madam: *we* might as well hope to be equal with the angels."

But, though as a rule too obvious to be worth expressing, this opinion does occasionally emerge into words. Katharina[1], the shrew who is "tamed" in so eminently masculine a manner by Petruchio, gives, when the process of subjection is complete, utterance to a series of apophthegms which are not likely to meet with full acceptance to-day:

> Thy husband is thy lord, thy life, thy keeper,
> Thy head, thy sovereign, one that cares for thee,

---

[1] I leave on one side the question of Shakspere's *sole* authorship of "The Taming of *the* Shrew," as also of his relation to "*A* Shrew."

> And craves no other tribute at thy hands
> But love, fair looks, and true obedience;
> Too little payment for so great a debt.
> Then vail your stomachs, for it is no boot,
> And place your hands below your husband's foot.

Perhaps of all the plays the one that most clearly illustrates this degrading view of marriage is *All's Well that Ends Well*. This play is based on one of Boccaccio's tales, and that not the most agreeable; but that it attracted Shakspere very remarkably is shown by the undoubted fact that he took with this play the special pains he took with but few of his others—he revised it, and largely re-wrote it, after some years. The additions and alterations are, in point of style, inferior to hardly anything he wrote; the play is full of wise thoughts admirably expressed; but it is tainted throughout with this vicious view of woman. Let us see if this is too harsh a judgment. Helena, who has been brought up as a dependent at the court of the Count of Rousillon, loves Bertram, the young Count, but the love is not returned. By her skill she cures the King of France of a painful disease. In return for this service the King promises to give her practically what she asks; whereon, with a daring to which all Shakspere's skill can hardly reconcile us, she demands that he should give her any husband she may ask. To this the King assents—and the whole tone of the play is to the effect that he was right to do so. Of course in this, as in so many others of his works, Shakspere is hampered by his original: he has to some extent to take his story as it comes before him; but it is noteworthy that the alterations he does make are not in the way of softening the monstrosity either of Helena's demand or of the King's consent. Marriage is again a mere farce, to be settled according to a whim. The fact that for once it is the man who is to suffer does not reconcile us to the painfulness of it all.

But while we indulge this pity for Bertram, let us notice that Helena's love for him is as slavish as that of Hero for Claudio or that of Silvia for Valentine. Representing, as Helena does, almost Shakspere's highest type of womanhood, she shows a capacity for action worthy of Portia, and a purity worthy of Imogen—but towards Bertram she is grovelling.

> My master, my dear lord he is, and I
> His servant live, and will his vassal die;

in fact she feels towards him as Katharina, when thoroughly tamed, feels towards Petruchio. "Indianlike, religious in her error, she adores the sun, that looks upon his worshipper, but knows of him no more." She is, indeed, patient Grisilde once again: and it is sufficient to say that it is a great blessing for the world that Grisildes, outside of plays and poems, are very rare.

The King is cured, and fulfils his vow. For the present our sympathies are all with Bertram, who at first indignantly refuses to accept his unwelcome wife, and afterwards, when compelled to do so, accepts her in the letter but not in the spirit, treats her with a contumely which rapidly loses for him the sympathy of the reader, and finally departs for the wars, leaving behind a promise to recognise her as his wife when a condition he believes impossible is fulfilled.

At the wars he rushes headlong into all kinds of debauchery, which ultimately enables Helena to fulfil his condition, but which unquestionably must lower him in her eyes. Of all noble qualities, indeed, he retains but courage; and of his downfall Helena knows. Yet, as we should expect after our previous experience of Shakspere's method, no sooner does he acknowledge his wrong-doing, or rather, no sooner does he, *without* acknowledging his wrong-doing, vow fidelity to Helena, than, fulfilling the title of the play, all ends well. For crudity and unsatisfactoriness this *dénoûment* is hard to beat; and yet, as we have seen, it is deliberate. As it stands, it is not Shakspere's hurried conclusion to satisfy the urgency of a stage-manager in want of novelties, but the carefully-wrought *second edition* of a play that had been on his hands for years. Here is a woman, represented as the noblest of her sex, seeking a husband by audacity verging on immodesty; welcoming each rebuff from her husband, each sting that emphatically bids her nor sit nor stand but go; taking advantage of his immoralities to slide into his favour; herself the purest of the pure, yet regardless of *his* impurity. Here, further, is a King, represented as noble, who simply plays with the happiness of his vassal, and forces him to marry a girl he never wishes to see again. Here, lastly, is a man, *ex hypothesi* worthy of Helena's love, who plunges, in order to avoid Helena, into the vilest sloughs of vice; and, with equal suddenness, accepts her affection and

renounces his way of life merely because, by an unexpected accident, she has been able to fulfil a condition
he thought impossible. Ascribe as much as you like of
this absurdity to Boccaccio; it remains that Shakspere
could not have taken the story as the basis of a play
unless, from the nature of his views on marriage, he
had failed to see how absurd it is.

In *Measure for Measure*, a still later and more mature
play, the absurdity, nay the atrocity, of this same theme
"boils up and bubbles till it positively o'er-runs the
stew." And that too in the very portion of the story
which Shakspere invented for himself and did not
borrow either from Cinthio or from Whetstone, the
original authorities for the main theme. The method
by which Angelo is outwitted is precisely the same as
that employed by Helena to capture Bertram: only, to
use the American phrase, "more so." That Mariana
should consent to such a plot, that Isabella should urge
it, that the Duke should sanction it, are three incredibles
knotted together into one absolute impossibility. But
almost worse, in this strange scene, is the Duke's punishment of Lucio—not for his atrocious libertinism, but
for the slanders with which he has wounded the Duke's
amour-propre. He is sentenced to a kind of marriage
which Lucio rightly calls worse than pressing to death,
whipping, and hanging; "slandering a prince," says the
Duke, "deserves all three." It has often been observed
that the last two Acts of *Measure for Measure* bear every
trace of having been written in a hurry. They do indeed
contrast marvellously with the astonishing power and

sympathy of the first three. But this rather strengthens
than weakens the argument we wish here to enforce.
Out of the abundance of the heart the mouth speaketh
when it is in a hurry; and the fact that in these hasty
scenes Shakspere again shows his degrading view of
marriage, reveals with absolute clearness how deeply
ingrained in his mind it was. When he had time, he
could elaborate a picture of marriage as noble as that
of Brutus and Portia; when he was compelled to write
quickly, he produces such caricatures as these we are
considering. He has often been censured for using
Death as a *deus ex machina* to unravel inextricable knots.
He deserves a much stronger censure for so constantly
bringing in Hymen to do the service of a scavenger.

A very similar censure must be passed on *Cymbeline*,
which, in spite of the gallant attempts of Gervinus and
others to rehabilitate it, we must regard as the play of
all Shakspere's which shows most genius deliberately
thrown to waste. Full as it is of beautiful passages and
idyllic scenes, it is yet tainted by this ineradicable vice
of contempt for women—and that though in Imogen
he has drawn one of the noblest pictures of women ever
seen. Let us for a moment, leaving the under-plots
and by-play on one side, glance at the main story.
Imogen, daughter of Cymbeline King of Britain, in
despite of her father's wish to marry her to his stepson
Cloten, gives her hand secretly to Posthumus, a " gentleman " of the stamp of Proteus and Bertram, who had
been reared at the court of the King. Adjectives are
piled up to describe the worth of Posthumus—he is a

man worth any woman; overbuys Imogen almost the sum he pays; compared with Cloten (no high eulogy, perhaps) he is an eagle to a puttock. The marriage is found out, and Posthumus is banished. As he leaves the shore, he waves glove, hat, and handkerchief to show how slowly his soul moves on, and how swiftly the ship. What does this paragon do as soon as he reaches Rome? He enters into a vile bet with a scoundrel named Iachimo about the honour of his wife. True, this incident is in Boccaccio, from whose novel Shakspere drew the story. But why did he take the story at all? Why did he not choose some nobler one? Why are we always to excuse him by blaming his authorities, when there were plenty of less degrading tales he might have selected had he chosen? This particular story, however, he *did* choose, and had to make the best of it.

Iachimo, whom we are inclined to think on the whole a worse villain than Iago himself, as he is certainly a more contemptible one, fails entirely in his attempts on Imogen. But he is enabled to put together a cock-and-bull story, and to back it up with material evidences, which though far weaker than those which betrayed Othello, might perhaps have justified Posthumus in making inquiries; though, as he knew Imogen and had good reason to know Iachimo, he might well have disbelieved them utterly from the first. He does nothing of the kind. With far less excuse than Othello, and indeed scarcely more than Leontes himself, he rushes at once into a belief in his wife's unfaithfulness, and in a burst of wild unreasoning fury threatens to tear her

"limb-meal." Had he done so aboveboard it would
have been hard to find excuses for him; but the plan
he actually concocts is so treacherous and contemptible
that to defend him would argue oneself indefensible.
He writes urging his wife to meet him at Milford
Haven, and suborns his servant to murder her on the
road. That she escapes this fate is due to the fact that
the servant Pisanio, in the few days' intercourse of the
journey, sees more deeply into her nature than his
master had seen in years of intimacy. The information
which to Posthumus was "proof as strong as his grief
and as certain as he expected his revenge," was to
Pisanio, at the first glance, "a slander whose edge was
sharper than the sword, whose tongue outvenomed all
the horrors of Nile." The prince of darkness is a gentleman indeed if Proteus, Bertram, or Posthumus deserves
the name.

But it is the consummation that really concerns us.
The play ends with a series of sudden conversions. Out
of every one of these convertites, to use the words of
Jaques, there is much matter to be heard and learned.
The stepmother confesses her machinations: Iachimo
is "glad to be constrained to utter that which torments
him to conceal," and confesses *his* share in the plot;
finally, Posthumus, who has already done some repentance, repents more vigorously still: whereupon
Imogen forgives him after the approved fashion, and
welcomes him to her bosom. "Hang there like fruit,
my soul," cries the happy husband, "till the tree die."
We have little guarantee that it will be long before he

again allows himself to be deceived. To reconcile us to this one improbability we have another. Cymbeline, having wasted many lives on the battle-field in order to resist Caesar's imposition of tribute, and having been victorious in the battle, agrees to pay the tribute nevertheless! Both of this reconciliation and of that of Posthumus and Imogen, we may say in the words that close the play:

> Never was a war did cease,
> Ere bloody hands were washed, with such a peace.

As we contemplate this farrago of repentances and pardons (even Iachimo coming in for his full share of both) we are tempted to parody Congreve's line, and to describe Shakspere's plays as made up of marrying in haste and repenting still more hastily.

There is surely no need to multiply examples. In *As You Like It* we have Celia falling in love with Oliver, who has hardly left his villany behind for a week. We say with Orlando, "Is it possible that on so little acquaintance you should like her? that but seeing you should love? and loving, woo? and wooing, she should grant? *and, will you persever?*" The answer must be that things like this happen in comedies. Others of the kind, indeed, happen in this very comedy. Not only does Rosalind love Orlando at first sight, but the case of Phebe and Silvius shows that in Shakspere's view the same law of matrimony holds in low life as in high. Phebe rejects Silvius; soon afterwards she falls in love with Ganymede, that is, with Rosalind: no sooner does she find out who Ganymede is, than she is perfectly

willing to marry the swain she had before refused even
with scorning. In *Twelfth Night*, written a year or two
after *As You Like It*, Sir Toby is probably the only
one who could give a reason for his marriage. In *Winter's
Tale*, perhaps the last play that Shakspere wrote of his
own accord, the chief weakness is this recurring fault
of a low view of the rights of women. In the *Merchant
of Venice*, as far as can be seen, Portia weds the most
contemptible of her suitors, a fellow who practically
owns that he seeks her for her wealth[1], and yet before
the caskets cants vigorously about the hard food of
Midas. What happened afterwards to these ill-assorted
couples had perhaps best be left to be decided by
Mr Punch's dramatic sequels. Fortunately marriage in
real life is not always so risky a business. To borrow
Pompilia's words on wedlock in general, "marriage in
Shakspere is after all but a counterfeit; a mere imitation
of the inimitable"; nor can even his stupendous genius
betray us into thinking that in this respect he has held
a true mirror up to nature.

[1] So, in the *Merry Wives*, Fenton seeks Anne Page for her seven hundred pounds
and what Sir Hugh Evans calls "possibilities" besides. Fenton has more brains than
his rival Slender, but he might, like Slender, have said that he "was freely dissolved,
and dissolutely," to marry Anne.

VII

Imaginative: 'The Witch of Atlas'

> For the authors of those great poems which we admire do not
> attain to excellence through the rules of any art; but they
> utter their beautiful melodies of verse in a state of inspiration,
> and, as it were, possessed by a spirit not their own.
> PLATO, *Ion*, Shelley's Translation.

THERE have always been, and probably always will
be, disputes as to the moral worth of Shelley's
life, and as to the value of his political and philosophical views; but as to the sincerity of his poetry
there can surely be no two opinions. Not only does that
poetry as a whole exemplify his conception of what
poetry should be, but it always expresses, as accurately
as was possible to his nature, what he saw and wished
his readers to see. No less than Dante or Wordsworth
did he scorn to put in an ornament for the sake of an
ornament, or to say what he did not think for the sake
of rounding off a paragraph or a poem.

Hence, when we find a poem that is specially difficult
of interpretation, we need not, in order to understand
it, seek among falsehoods or mere prettiness. We do
not believe, as some do, that Shelley ever wrote a poem
without definite meaning—that is, we believe that at
the moment when the enthusiasm was upon him he
saw with absolute distinctness the succession of images
that passed before his eyes. Mr Stopford Brooke will
have it that the *Witch of Atlas* is "a poem in which he
sent his imagination out like a child into a meadow,

without any aim save to enjoy itself. Now and again,"
says Mr Brooke, "Shelley himself alters or arranges the
manner of the sport, as if with some intention, but
never so much as to spoil the natural wildness of the
Imagination's play. 'I mean nothing,' Shelley would
have said; 'I did not write the poem. My imagination
made it of its own accord'." This is true in one sense;
but it is false if it means that Shelley, while the poem's
grip was on him, did not see its pictures clearly, whatever may have been the case as they faded. Even its
jests express the truth as Shelley saw it, and its very
dreams are real *as dreams*. Shelley indeed, as anyone
who has read his fragmentary *Speculations on Meta-
physics* knows, had no necessity to go beyond his own
experience for the visions of an Alastor or a Prince
Athanase; his actual dreams were potent enough without his inventing others. It has often been observed,
similarly, that his descriptions of mountains, seas, and
lakes, as given in his poems, are but versifications of
the descriptions he had given to his friends in his letters;
and in the same way the rocks, rivers, and caverns of
his mystical verses correspond, sometimes minutely,
to what he had actually seen in the visionary journeys
on which his soul so often set forth. Even if the veiled
eye of memory could not reproduce them, the sub-
conscious soul was assured of their reality. To use the
words he applies to the melancholy of Prince Athanase,
they are

the shadow of a dream
Which, through the soul's abyss, like some dark stream,

> Through shattered mines and caverns underground,
> Rolls, shaking its foundations.

The letters of Shelley again and the reports of his friends show that there is no philosophy expressed in his verse which he was not willing to defend in prose: and outside of the *Cenci* it would be hard to find in his works a single opinion uttered in which he did not literally believe.

Further, the range of his ideas, though wide, is limited. Amid endless varieties of detail, he repeats the same landscapes, denounces the same evils, hazards the same conjectures, and dreams the same dreams. Hence, to interpret an obscure poem, we need not search beyond the borders of Shelley's realm as we know it. He is always himself, and always ranging over the same country. Few poets have developed more wonderfully, and yet his earliest poems are like his latest, and his noblest lyrics touch on the same themes as his worst. *Queen Mab* helps to explain the *Prometheus*; *Alastor* has not a little in common with *Prince Athanase*; and there is much in *Laon and Cythna* which throws light upon the *Triumph of Life*. To take but one example of this sameness—we find everywhere in Shelley the same favourite symbolisms recurring again and again. Whatever poem we open, we light upon pavilions, crystalline spheres, mountains and fountains, pinions and dominions, wastes and wildernesses, camelopards, antelopes, and alligators; the earth is daedal, sorcerers are Archimages; we walk beneath the folding star, and tread upon wind-flowers; while behind every tree we see

more nymphs and satyrs than vast earth can hold. Some
of these words are indistinct in their symbolism, and
mean different things at different times; others have
attained a comparative fixity, and the interpretation of
them in one passage will suit another. But every
symbol, at the particular time, is clearly seen and truly
described.

Thus, in approaching what is perhaps the most obscure of all his poems, the *Witch of Atlas*, we are not
without our guiding principles. The poem is not a mere
play of fancy; it represents a truth as Shelley saw it.
And, secondly, we shall probably find that truth expressed with more or less fulness elsewhere in his
writings. Nor have we far to seek for that other expression of the truth. Looking at his *Defence of Poetry*, we
find the following passage: "Poetry turns all things to
loveliness; it exalts the beauty of that which is most
beautiful, and it adds beauty to that which is most
deformed; it marries exultation and horror, grief and
pleasure, eternity and change; it subdues to union under
its light yoke all irreconcilable things. It transmutes
all that it touches, and every form moving within the
radiance of its presence is changed by wondrous sympathy to an incarnation of the spirit which it breathes;
its secret alchemy turns to potable gold the poisonous
waters which flow from death through life; it strips
the veil of familiarity from the world, and lays bare the
naked and sleeping beauty, which is the spirit of its
forms."

That everything which is here said to be the function

of poetry is also the function of the Witch could be
easily shown did space permit; it is sufficient to compare
with the last sentence in the passage just quoted a single
verse from the poem:

> To her eyes
> The naked beauty of the soul lay bare,
> And often through a rude and worn disguise
> She saw the inner form most bright and fair:
> And then she had a charm of strange device,
> Which, murmured on mute lips with tender tone,
> Could make that spirit mingle with her own.

That, in fact, the Witch is Poetry has been seen by
many readers. It is not likely that Mr Stopford Brooke
was the first to discern a hint of the poem in a line
from *Mont Blanc*—·

> In the still cave of the witch Poesy;

and indeed it is surprising that so obvious a truth should
have escaped the eyes of any attentive student of
Shelley. Some, indeed, may have felt a kind of super-
stitious dread of discovering the secret which Shelley
himself had laid under a ban:

> If you unveil my Witch, no priest or primate
> Can shrive you of that sin;

but the sin has been dared by many, and will be dared
by many more.

The Witch is Poetry; but, of course, she is Poetry in
the sense in which Shelley understood the word, the
sense explained in the *Defence*. To him, Rousseau,
Raphael and Bacon were poets equally with Dante and

K S   8

Milton; an action might be poetry as truly as a line of Virgil. The death of Regulus was a poem; the stubborn resistance of Rome to Hannibal was an epic. Both alike were inspired with the scorn of the finite which is of the very essence of poetry. Hence there is naturally some divergence in the words chosen by different commentators as best expressing the Witch. While Mr Stopford Brooke calls the Witch Poetry simply, Mr W. B. Yeats, not less correctly, calls her Beauty, and refers us thereby to *The Hymn to Intellectual Beauty* for some at least of the explanatory parallels. We ourselves, for reasons which will be more clearly seen in the sequel, prefer the name Creative Imagination. "Poetry," says Shelley, in the same *Defence* which we have already quoted, "creates anew the universe after it has been annihilated in our minds by the recurrence of impressions blunted by reiteration. It justifies the bold and true words of Tasso, *Non merita nome di creatore, se non Iddio ed il Poeta*—none deserves the name of creator but God and the poet." It is true that the word *creative* is here used in a special sense. Inspiration is in one very important aspect receptive merely; the poet must wait for his hours of enthusiasm, and when they come must obey the impulse. It is imagination which casts its images on the mind of the poet; and his imagination but reflects those images, while it afterwards recollects them and then throws them into what we call poetic form. Poetry feeds, in a wise passiveness, on the eternal visions presented to it from the everlasting spirit, and he is the best poet who puts the least of self into his poems. This is true; and we must never lose sight of the fact that Shelley, after the fashion of his beloved Spinoza, drew a distinction between the Universal Imagination and its particular manifestations in individuals. Poetry, says Shelley, "is not subject to the control of the active powers of the mind." Nevertheless, as she receives her material direct from the creative powers of the universe, and, however passively, reacts upon it, she may well be called herself creative. The vision projected upon her eye by the great Substance is infinitely intense, but it is for that very reason obscure; and she must, in reproducing it, exercise her creative powers in relieving the obscurity.

The Witch, then, is under one symbol what Schiller's "Maiden from Afar" is under another:

> And blessed was her presence there—
> Each heart, expanding, grew more gay;
> Yet something loftier still than fair
> Kept man's familiar looks away.
>
> From fairy gardens, known to none,
> She brought mysterious fruits and flowers,
> The things of some serener sun,
> Some Nature more benign than ours.

As with Schiller's maiden, too, we shall detect in her a certain hesitation between the particular and the universal aspects. Sometimes—to borrow once more the phraseology of Spinoza—she seems to be Imagination as one of the infinite attributes of the Divine; sometimes she is Imagination as limited into a finite mode; sometimes she seems to be both at once. But through-

8–2

out, whether universal or particular, she is the creator
of new materials of knowledge, and power, and pleasure;
she comprehends all science, and is that to which all
science must be referred. A poem, says Shelley elsewhere, is the very image of life expressed in its
eternal truth; it is, as Spinoza would say, *essentia
vitae sub specie aeternitatis*; and, as the transmitter of
a poem, a poet was to Shelley what he was to our
old English ancestors, to Dunbar, and to Carlyle, emphatically a Maker. He did not believe, like Browning,
that man since he is a created being is "compelled to
grow, not make in turn, yet forced to try and make,
else fail to grow." The inspired man both grows and
makes.

From the *Witch of Atlas*, then, if only we can interpret
it, we shall learn even more clearly what Shelley's view
of Imagination is, than we can from the fragmentary
Defence of Poetry, noble and amazingly penetrating as
that essay is. For Shelley's view of poetry was such
that poetry alone could convey it; when it is described
in prose, half the mystic glory swims away. Its appeal
is not to the mind, but to that which is above and
beyond the mind; to the certainties which cannot be
proved; and even the explanation of which is beyond
the power of prose.

With this idea ever present to our minds, we may
begin our study of the poem. The first conception of
the Witch as a just type of Imagination doubtless came
to Shelley from reading those lines in the fourth book
of the *Aeneid*, in which Dido speaks to her sister of the

priestess who, as she believes, can either restore Aeneas
to her, or loose her from the chain of his love.

> Nigh rising Atlas, next the falling sun,
> Long tracts of Aethiopian climates run;
> There a Massylian priestess I have found,
> Honoured for age, for magic arts renowned:
> The Hesperian temple was her trusted care;
> 'Twas she supplied the wakeful dragon's fare:
> She poppy-seeds in honey taught to steep,
> Reclaimed his rage, and soothed him into sleep.
> ....Her charms unbind
> The chains of love, or fix them on the mind;
> She stops the torrents, leaves the channel dry,
> Repels the stars, and backward bears the sky.

This priestess is one of the Atlantides—the three
Hesperian maidens, daughters of Atlas, who guarded
the sacred apples. Her powers are precisely those
ascribed to Orpheus, and, as Shelley read the lines, he
would inevitably think of the magic skill of the Thracian
bard, until the symbol of the witch stood in his mind
for poetic imagination. That this is so, is made still
more probable by the reference in the eleventh stanza
to the rude kings of pastoral Garamant; for this same
fourth book of the *Aeneid* is full of the Garamantian
tribes, and contains more than one reference to the rude
king Iarbas, *Ammone satus, rapta Garamantide nympha*.
With this symbol thus established in his mind, and
ready at any moment to emerge into complete consciousness, Shelley made that ascent of Monte San Pellegrino
which, as his wife tells us, suggested the poem to him,
and indeed so filled him with its main ideas that he
finished it in the following three days. The poem begins

by asserting the priority of the Imagination to the cruel
twins Error and Truth (*i.e.* Fact). Mistake and Accuracy
are alike possible only to mere Reason, such as that
which is ascribed even to Locke, Hume and Gibbon.
A sophister or calculator may be wrong or he may be
correct; for he deals with phenomena in Time, which
Shelley had learnt from Spinoza to be only a phantasm.
Essential Truth is visible only to the Imagination,
which alone is the worthy faculty of the poet. All this
is expressed by Shelley in the words:

> Those cruel twins whom at a birth
> Incestuous Change bore to her father Time,
> Error and Truth, had hunted from the earth
> All those bright natures which adorned its prime,
> And left us nothing to believe in, worth
> The pains of putting into learned rhyme.

Parallels to this can be found everywhere in Shelley's
poetry; it is sufficient to refer here to the famous passage
in *Epipsychidion*:

> Love...is like thy light,
> Imagination, which from earth and sky,
> And from the depths of human phantasy,
> As from a thousand prisms and mirrors, fills
> The Universe with glorious beams and kills
> Error, the worm, with many a sun-like beam
> Of its reverberated lightning;

where, however, Shelley is not so much concerned, as
here, to distinguish between the Imagination and the
Understanding, and therefore represents Imagination
as slaying the Error which here he regards as altogether
non-existent in her world.

Severed thus from Reason, the Witch, we are told, lived on Atlas Mountain. This is because Imagination scales the heavens and holds communion with the stars; and Atlas, as Virgil tells us, swirls on his shoulder the pole of heaven with all its train of blazing constellations. She lives in a cavern by a secret fountain. Caverns and fountains are common enough in Shelley's poetry. We are reminded here of that cave to which, as he tells us in *Epipsychidion*, he was led by the Moon-like lady of his dreams; a cavern in the midst of the obscure forest of the world, through which flew the twin babes, Life and Death. And we are also reminded of the fountains from which came the voice of the enchanted being whom he pursued so long in vain. But there is no need to use any words but those of Mr Yeats: "So good a Platonist as Shelley could hardly have thought of any cave as a symbol, without thinking of Plato's cave that was the world; and so good a scholar may well have had Porphyry on the Cave of the Nymphs in his mind. When I compare Porphyry's description of the cave where the Phaeacian boat left Odysseus with Shelley's description of the cave of the Witch...I find it hard to think otherwise." Thus the cavern is the type of the world in general, and specially of the world in its mysterious and occult aspect; it is Mother Earth as the source of magic power.

Whatever this cave may be, the Witch is not, like us dull mortals, shut up within it. From it flows a river, whose source is in one place called secret and in another sacred; from which the camelopard, the serpent and all beasts drink reviving and soothing draughts. This stream runs like life through all the realms of knowledge—knowledge and life being to Shelley, like Thought and Extension to Spinoza, but two aspects of the same thing. All things, he says in the *Defence*, exist as they are perceived, at least in relation to the percipient; and he quotes Milton's famous lines:

> The mind is its own place and in itself
> Can make a heaven of hell, a hell of heaven.

He did not, it is true, believe the essence of the world to be mind. It is, as he tells us more than once, a painted veil, which those who live call life; and unreal shapes are painted upon it; it is neither reason nor imagination, but something that includes both—and more akin to the latter. Yet to Shelley life and perception were one. Thus the river is in one aspect Thought, in another Time; it is a fleeting, flowing thing, behind which lies a reality we cannot conceive. Down this river Alastor sailed, in search of his unattainable ideal:

> O stream,
> Whose source is inaccessibly profound,
> Whither do thy mysterious waters tend?
> *Thou imagest my life.*

Down such a stream flows the everlasting Universe of Things—as we are told in *Mont Blanc*. Down this same river, as we shall see, floats our Witch, in her magic boat, that moves like the winged thought of Homer, on the voyage which is to be so full of blessing to mortals. Doubtless, also, Shelley had in mind the mountain of Helicon on which the Muses dwell, the caves of that mountain, and the Permessian waters that flow down its sides. The fountain is secret, not only because the origin of life is hidden from us, but because in ancient symbolism knowledge, and especially occult knowledge, is derived from hidden waters. If Shelley had only known the *Edda*, he would have referred us to Odin and the well of Mimir.

We have already seen why Shelley makes the mother of the Witch one of the three Atlantides, daughters of Atlas, that watch the golden apples of beauty and knowledge in the garden of the Hesperides. Her father is the Sun, the creative principle of life. In *Epipsychidion*, the Vision that Shelley so long sought in vain is at last discovered, and is found to be

> Soft as an incarnation of the Sun
> When light is changed to love;

that is, the Intellectual Beauty (in this place symbolised as the Witch) is, when embodied in a human form, an incarnation of the creative principle; when regarded as pervasive and eternal, she is a daughter of that principle, and of course reproduces the lineaments of her father.

The all-beholding Sun, his light being changed to love, sees the beauty of the Hesperian nymph, and kisses her to dissolution. She is changed into a vapour, into a cloud, into a meteor, into an invisible star—for Imagination, regarded as a thing apart from creative power, is vague, fleeting, and transitory. The offspring of the Sun—the Imagination informed with the creative omnipotence—is immortal, unchangeable, and gifted with all the magic that dwells in her sire. At first a dewy splendour, she takes shape and motion, and becomes an embodied power—her body, of course, being that spiritual body with which Shelley's thoughts are so often dowered. Garmented in the light of her own beauty; her eyes as deep—to use the comparison which has drawn the admiration of Francis Thompson—as two openings of night seen through the roof of a tempest cloven by the lightning; her hair dark, like the trail of a comet far beyond human ken, she is worthy of her parentage. Like Circe she is the Sun's true daughter; the cave grows warm with her presence. Like Circe she controls all beasts, and weaves magic things with her spindle; like Circe she is beautiful. Another Orpheus, she draws animals after her, and tames them to her will, giving courage to the timid, and gentleness to the savage: *emollit mores, nec sinit esse feros*. Old Silenus, Dryope, and Faunus follow her; for the wildest and most vulgar fancies, when touched with true Imagination, are transformed into unaccustomed beauty. Universal Pan unites himself with the Lady—for the universe is created by the Imagination, and does not exist without her—all things exist as they are perceived. God himself in creating the world, as Milton tells us, beholds it as answering his great Idea; and apart from that Idea it cannot be.

At first, it is true, the Imagination, working in ignorant and untrained minds, produces grotesque and quaint fancies. She is pursued by the rude kings of Garamant, by pygmies and Polyphemes, and by lumps neither alive nor dead, dog-headed, bosom-eyed, and bird-footed. These are the creations of an uncultivated imagination, such as gave birth to the art of Egypt or of India, and such as was speedily rejected by the Greeks and their followers in favour of a tamed and refined form of the faculty. Nevertheless even grotesqueness, so far as it is creative, has a true nobility.

In the face of Imagination, what we call reality is dimmed. As soon as she is seen, all thoughts are fixed upon her. "Vice," says Pope,

> is a monster of so frightful mien
> As, to be hated, needs but to be seen;

the exact contrary is the case with the Witch—to see her is to love her. But there is some danger in her very beauty. As with Moses when he descended from the mount after communion with Jahweh, her face is too glorious to be gazed upon without dazzling our eyes. She must be veiled; and accordingly she takes her spindle, and weaves three threads of fleecy light, such as the dawn may kindle the clouds with, and these, we are told in a remarkable phrase, are a shadow for the splendour of her love. For, as we shall see later, Shelley recognised no distinction between the Intellectual Beauty that informs the world and that sustaining Love which holds it together.

The web is woven of fleecy mist, and of lines of light, because, as Shelley believed, the Imagination at its highest shuns the definite. Its edges are never sharp and clear; it deals with dreams, with shadows, with clouds; it has nothing to do with "this solidity and compound mass." Its very brightness often brings obscurity; "dark with excess of bright its skirts appear." It is inevitable that the infinite ocean should fade into shadow toward the horizon; and the rim of the sun is blurred as he sinks in glory to his setting.

The next few stanzas (14–20) illustrate the comprehensiveness of the ideas which, in the view of Shelley, were included under the word Imagination. We have already seen how widely in the *Defence of Poetry* he had stretched that word, and here we see the same thing yet more clearly. The dwelling of the Lady is odorous, and odours are kept in a kind of aviary to stir sweet thoughts or sad in destined minds. We are reminded of the verse in the *Sensitive Plant*, which tells of

> The hyacinth purple, and white, and blue,
> Which flung from its bells a sweet peal anew
> Of music so delicate, soft, and intense,
> It was felt like an odour within the sense;

and to Shelley odours were not only, as they are to most of us, the potent arousers of memory, but also a form of music and a vehicle of Love. As much as the Dorian mood of flutes and soft recorders could they stir heroes to battle, or chase away anguish and doubt, and fear, and sorrow, and pain from mortal or immortal minds. Once more, in the cavern are Visions, swift and quaint, each in its pale sheath like a chrysalis, ready to bear their message to those whom Shelley, perhaps unconsciously following Chaucer, calls the saints of Love.

This is another intimation of that mystic union of
Poetry with Love, which was to Shelley, as to his
masters Plato and Dante, the very first principle in the
imaginative interpretation of the world. Just as, in the
Prometheus, the character of Asia stands for that Love
which must lie at the back of all social regeneration,
so here we are taught the converse truth that without
Imagination Love is sordid and unholy; in fact that in
proportion as a lover is a poet so is his love lofty.
Deprived of the love of human beings, as Shelley tells
us in one of his striking fragments, the poetic mind
loves the flowers, the grass, and the waters, and the sky.
In the motion of the very leaves of spring, in the blue
air, there is then found a secret correspondence with
our heart. There is eloquence in the tongueless wind,
and a melody in the flowing brooks and the rustling of
the reeds beside them, which, by their inconceivable
relation to something within the soul, awaken the spirits
to a dance of breathless rapture, and bring tears of
mysterious tenderness to the eyes, like the enthusiasm
of patriotic success, or the voice of one beloved singing
to you alone.

Not far removed from this idea is that presented in
stanza 18 just below. The cavern, like the house of
Alma in the *Faerie Queene*, is stored with scrolls of
strange device, the works of some Saturnian Archimage,
which tell how the golden age may be restored. Social
amelioration is to be found only by imaginative sympathy
with the lot of others. He who can adequately picture
to himself the state of the poor will be cured of the

lust of gold; he who can picture beforehand a battle
will be cured of the lust of blood; the oppressor is he
who cannot *feel* himself the oppressed. On the other
hand, the apparently untamable forces of revolution
will obey the spell of Imagination. Jupiter, in the
Prometheus Unbound, is right when he says that his
Enemy, even when he hangs, seared by the long revenge
on Caucasus, would not doom the tyrant to eternal
anguish; for he can well picture woe. And, lest we
should forget the real meaning of Imagination, the
stanza we are studying ends with identifying the scrolls
of the Archimage with the inmost lore of love.

> *Amore e il cor gentil sono una cosa.*

Yet further, the next stanza tells us that even the most
mechanical inventions, and even the dullest discoveries
of science, owe their life to this same power. Touched
by the sun of creative intelligence, they shine

> In their own golden beams; each like a flower
> Out of whose depth a firefly shakes his light
> Under a cypress in a starless night.

At first the Lady lives alone; before Imagination has
time to create her own companions she is in a loneliness
which is scarcely to be distinguished from non-existence.
She is, indeed, in the same utter solitude as that in
which we may conceive God to have lived before the
Creation—a solitude, however, rich with the potentiality
of all being. Her own thoughts, without material upon
which to work, fly rapidly to and fro, and speedily build
for her that universe on which she in turn employs her

thoughts. But this very world is fleeting; while she is building she is destroying; the mountains and the trees begin to die from the moment of their birth. The boundless ocean itself will be consumed like a drop of dew; the stubborn earth (in Shaksperean language the *centre*) must be scattered like a cloud. But she cannot die as they do. For, as Spinoza says, although the mind can only imagine anything or remember what is past, while the body endures, yet it cannot be absolutely destroyed with the body, but something of it remains that is eternal. Thus the Lady cannot permit the Oreads and Naiads to remain with her as her satellites; and yet she will make her paths in the streams in which they dwell. The Imagination differs from God in this, that while she can create a world, that world is tinged with a weakness borrowed from her. To God the world is eternal; but to us, though we are creators, the world must be mortal as we are; and yet something of us remains that is eternal, and this, says Shelley, is the power possessed by the Imagination of endlessly re-creating its images.

Apart from this power in us, not only is the world non-existent, but the past is dead. It is not learning that reconstructs the past, but the imaginative faculty. The historian must be a poet, or he is no historian. The true chroniclers are those who, in the Witch's cavern, spell out the scrolls of dread antiquity—but add some grace, caught from her, to the wrought poesy; while the odours of memory, wrought into a blaze by the fire of genius (stanzas 26 and 27), cast true light

upon the past. Men scarcely realise how beautiful that
fire is; and yet it must not be the dry light of science;
it has to be veiled and dimmed by the very Imagination
that raises it. A literal transcript of the past—a photo-
graph of it—is *ipso facto* false; to see it true one must
look at it through the mist of romance. "Fiction that
makes fact alive is fact too"—and here Shelley and
Browning would be at one; but Shelley would have
added, Fact, without some fiction in it, is not fact at
all. For a similar reason, in the next stanza Shelley
tells us that the Lady, though never sleeping, lies in
trance within the fountain; she views things, after all,
as they are refracted in the waves of life.

In the *Prometheus Unbound*, we are told that at the
moment of the great transformation, the Spirit of the
Earth

> hid herself
> Within a fountain in the public square,
> Where she lay like the reflex of the moon
> Seen in a wave under green leaves;

and from thence beheld the ugly human shapes trans-
form themselves into mild and lovely forms, while the
halcyons fed unharmed on night-shade. But here the
meaning seems to be somewhat different; the passage
appears to wish to emphasise the fact that pure Imagination is useless to mankind; and Shelley, to whom, as he
said to Peacock, poetry was very subordinate to moral
and political science, would not have spent a single
stanza on Imagination except as human. But the
Imagination, human as it is, must be distorted neither

by passion nor by reason. The Lady must lie as in sleep, inaccessible to the tumult of the work-a-day world, and must at all hazards keep her contemplations calm. When the storms arise, she must seek refuge within the well of fire that is to be found amid the meadows of asphodel—*i.e.* in the life of thought that is only to be found in that region where all warriors rest from battle, like Achilles after the wars of windy Troy.

The means by which she speaks to men is poetry—poetry in the narrower sense as the word is generally understood. She travels down the river of Life in a boat—as Alastor travelled, as Laon and Cythna travelled, on their endless quest. The image is old: it was the very one hit upon by the Icelandic skalds, who called Poetry Odin's boat; by Chaucer, who in *Troilus* tells us that "in the see the boot hath swich travayle of his conning that unnethe he can stere it"; by Dante in *Purgatorio, la navicella del mio ingegno*; by Propertius, *non est ingenii cumba gravanda tui*, and in fact by almost all poets. The symbolic origin of this boat, however, has never been so fully illustrated as by Shelley. It was, say some, wrought for Venus by Vulcan—that is, it was fashioned by fiery genius for the messages of Love. Or else it sprang from a seed sown by Love in the star of Venus—by which figure the exquisite spontaneity of lyric verse is beautifully emphasised. And to Shelley Poetry that was not lyric had scarcely any claim to the name; nor has Poetry anything to deal with but Love. As Professor Bradley puts it, "Whatever in the world has any worth is an expression of Love. Love sometimes talks. Love talking musically is Poetry."

Without Imagination Poetry is naught. It is the Witch that breathes into it the breath of life—as the Creator breathed life into the nostrils of Adam. But, as to Hamlet the art of acting, in its very frenzy, must beget a kind of temperance, so with the noble mania of Poetry. Poetry is wild beauty tamed—like a panther at the feet of Bacchus, or a flame subdued to the service of Vesta's hearth. So marked is this feature of it, that Shelley uses to describe it one of those reversed comparisons of which he is so fond. The symbol is like the thing symbolised; the boat is like a winged thought of Homer. So, in the *Prometheus*, Shelley compares an avalanche to the movement of a Revolutionary thought; and so, in *Mont Blanc*, he compares the course of the Arve to the flowing of the universe through the mind. Whenever this occurs in Shelley, it denotes extreme earnestness.

The pilot of the boat is a sexless thing, tempered with liquid Love out of fire and snow—for Love can reconcile all things, and all high truth is the reconciliation of opposites. This Hermaphrodite is, in fact, "Lyric Love, half angel and half bird, and all a wonder and a wild desire." With it, the Lady glides down the stream, which is Life conceived as Mind, until she reaches the austral waters, that seem ocean, beyond the fabulous Thamondocana (a name borrowed from Ptolemy), which represents the Universal Mind, or rather that Essential Substance, beyond and including

Mind, which in Shelley's view represented the real truth of things. That lake is only to be perceived in reposeful contemplation, for it is itself the negation of all tumult. There, whatever storms may rage, is the calm haven in which the Imagination can do its work undisturbed. "Port after stormie seas, death after life, does greatly please."

At this point (stanza 51), where we may with some plausibility guess that Shelley began his third day's work upon the poem, the tone changes. Hitherto it has been serious; it now becomes light. Doubtless the change was in part due to a change in the poet's own mood; but partly also to a deliberate desire to represent an aspect of Imagination which is easily overlooked. The Imagination that goes to a humorous creation like Falstaff, or to a grotesque creation like Caliban, is fully as great as that which goes to *Lear* or to the *Divine Comedy*. Nay (stanza 54) in some points Imagination may even borrow from Rumour herself. She is now comic and now tragic; now her sphere is laughter and now pathos. At other times, again, it is pure poetry, without any definite quality, such as that of Shelley himself in *Life of Life* or in the very *Witch of Atlas* which we are considering; it is such poetry as Arion may have sung when he was borne on the waves by the dolphin. Such poetry is that which, like so much of Byron and Shelley, is pure description; when the poet describes a crag or a storm for its own sake, then the Witch is running upon the platforms of the wind, or climbing the steepest ladder of the crudded rack.

Of course, in reducing Shelley's symbols to their
lowest terms, one runs more than a risk of destroying
the poetry altogether; I am not unmindful of the
warning so admirably given by Mr Yeats as to inter-
preting *Prometheus Unbound* as simply Godwin's *Political
Justice* put into rhyme. To the learned scholar who said
that Shelley was a crude revolutionist, Mr Yeats quoted
the lines which tell how the halcyons ceased to prey on
fish, and how poisonous leaves became good for food,
to show that he foresaw more than any political regeneration. Of the *Witch of Atlas*, as much as of the *Prometheus*, are Mrs Shelley's words true: " It requires a mind
as subtle and penetrating as his own to understand the
mystic meanings scattered throughout the poem. They
elude the ordinary reader by their abstraction and
delicacy of distinction, but they are far from vague."
All this is very true. A political regeneration divorced
from Intellectual Beauty would have seemed to Shelley
no regeneration at all; and Intellectual Beauty cannot
be put into words even if those words were as ethereal
as his own. Nevertheless the converse is true, that
Imagination and Intellectual Beauty had to Shelley a
practical and social value. They are as useful as reasoning
and mechanics; and a poet, no less than a bridge-maker
or a politician, has his solid use in the State. Nay,
without Imagination, all political effort is vain. "Poetry,"
says Shelley in a remarkable passage in the *Defence*, "is
the faculty which contains within itself the seeds at
once of its own and of social renovation." It was the
poetry in the authors of the Christian religion which

was the secret of the success that religion has had; it was the poetry in the chivalric system which refined the manners of the Middle Ages. Even when society is decaying, Poetry ever addresses itself to those faculties which are the last to be destroyed, and its voice is heard, like the footsteps of Astraea, departing from the world. As long as there is in a nation susceptibility to poetic pleasure, that nation is not utterly corrupt.

This being the view of Shelley as to the relation between poetry and politics, we are not in the least surprised to find some very practical politics in the *Witch of Atlas*; and the last part of the poem is devoted to describing, with a touch of ironical humour, this aspect of the Witch's work. Her chief sport is to glide down old Nilus, from the steep of utmost Axume, by Maeris and the Mareotid lake, past the Labyrinth and the Pyramids, to the sea. These represent old civilisations, with all their triumphs of mechanical skill, and all the unmentionable horrors of their lawless laws and customary codes. Man, whose life ought to move on in a smooth stream, like the Nile over the plains of the Delta, finds himself disturbed by the hideous strife due to the distorted terrors induced by priestcraft and the wrongs of secular oppressors. We, says Shelley, must take an unpiloted and a starless course over the wild surface, to an unknown goal; but she in the calm depths. The piercing eye of Imagination can see, in the dreadful present, the promise of a glorious future; and, with something of the calm of a Spinoza or a Goethe, the philosopher can watch the agonising world move on to

her destined end. The Witch can gaze at princes en-
joying their undeserved luxury, and at peasants in their
huts; she can see the priests asleep, all educated into
a dull and useless uniformity, and the sailors on the
waves, and the dead in their eternal slumber. To her calm
eyes the naked beauty of the soul lies bare. And she
has a charm that robs the poverty-struck life of its
sordidness, and dulls the edge of care. This is that
dream-like Hope which comes to all, and keeps the
world for ever young. For lack of this charm, Tithonus
grew old, and withered into a grey shadow; and it was
for lack of it that Adonis died despite the prayers of
Venus. For what would life be without its dreams? It
is they that lend romance to the most humdrum of
existences, and touch the dreariest heart with a glowing
ray from Infinitude. It is they that teach us the secret
of Love—a secret which the Lady does not know at
first, but which she will learn in time; and when she
learns it, the Imagination will attain its true perfection.

As Imagination penetrates into the brains of men,
they see the futility of their crimes. Elsewhere Shelley
tells us that a mountain, if duly understood by Imagination, has power to repeal whole codes of fraud and
wrong; and here, in other words, he says the same.
Under the influence of Imagination, the miser, a new
Zacchaeus, restores his gains; the lying scribe confesses
his falsehoods, the priest owns that his religion was a
fraud carried on for the sake of lucre. Nay, kings themselves renounce the trappings of royalty, and reveal
kingship to the world as a grotesque and indecent sham.

Soldiers, once given the power to see their trade as it really is, rush forth to beat their swords into plough-shares; for war is not possible as soon as the point of view of one's opponents is grasped. For the same reason, the gaolers release from prison the liberal captives, whose attitude to life they realise; for as soon as we see that there is something to be said for a creed, we can no longer try to crush it by force. Shelley, by the way, is guilty here both of a false quantity and of a more serious inconsistency. King Amǎsis, who should really be King Amāsis, is much annoyed at the release of the schismatics. But, if he had been sufficiently imaginative to dress an ape up in his crown and robes, he would not have minded a few liberals in his realm.

From political freedom we are led on to free love. True wisdom, says Shelley, would see no ill in lovers who had obeyed the impulses of Nature. *Tout comprendre, c'est tout pardonner*; and complete comprehension is possible only to the imaginative mind.

Lastly, if there is anything higher than love, it is friendship. At least Sidney, Michael Angelo, and Shakspere seem to have thought so. And of all evil souls the worst is that which finds pleasure in sundering friendships; while to restore the broken union is perhaps the hardest, as it is the noblest, task in the world. "I should like," says Jean Paul, "to be present at all reconciliations; for there is no love that moves us like returning love." The task is hard indeed, but it is not beyond the power of the Witch. A determined effort to imagine oneself into the position of the other mind can succeed, where all else fails. With visions clear of deep affection and of truth sincere she unites the friends once more.

At the end of the *Utopia* Sir Thomas More recurs to the tone of irony which, in the enchantment of his dreams, he had for a time forgotten. "There are many things in the Republic of Nowhere which I rather wish than hope to see adopted in England." Similarly, having surveyed the work of his Witch, so noble and so exalted, Shelley recurs to the fleeting tone he had for a while discarded. These wondrous doings are pranks; this immortal benefactor of the human race is a mere eccentric; no sensible person, with comfortable things all around him, and the summer sun shedding pleasant rays upon him, can possibly believe in her existence or her doings. But it is just from such common sense that Shelley does his utmost to deliver us. The rest of the acts of the Witch, and all that she did, says he, are not to be told on these garish summer days, in which we believe scarce more than we can see—to Shelley the worst of restrictions. The full story must be reserved for a weird winter night—for then the Imagination has full play. As he had already sung in the *Hymn to Intellectual Beauty*:

> There is a harmony
> In autumn, and a lustre in its sky,
> Which through the summer is not heard nor seen;

and those who have read and loved the *Witch of Atlas* will agree with the lines in *Marianne's Dream*:

> Sleep has sights as clear and true
> As any waking eyes can view.

VIII

The Plastic Stress

ABSOLUTE philosophical consistency is neither to be expected nor to be desired in poetry. When poets have endeavoured to give to their works the exactitude of a *Critique of Pure Reason*, or even that of a *Manual of Practical Farming*, they have usually spoilt the poem without advancing the cause of knowledge. We read Lucretius and Wordsworth, for example, with most pleasure when they forget the didactic and allow the impulse of their genius free play; and even the *Georgics* is less delightful than usual when it deviates into the actual teaching of agriculture.

Nevertheless, a certain measure of philosophy is perhaps almost a necessary element in true poetry. We say this without forgetting the simple narrative charm of the *Odyssey*, or the captivating *naïveté* of several of Herrick's songs, or the claim of Morris to be regarded as but the idle singer of an empty day. All rules have their exceptions; but it may fairly be maintained that as faith without works is dead, so a poem without *some* touch either of solid fact or of deep speculation is likely to have but a short life. The technical theology in Dante or in Milton may be a source of weakness, and of weakness the more marked in proportion to the apparent continuity and rotundity of the thought; but

Dante or Milton entirely without theology would hardly have written poetry at all. Their views, rigid and harsh as they were, provided just that centre of stability around which their idealism and imagination could set: without them, their vision would have been misty and their heavens cloudy. Similarly, even with such a poet as Spenser, while it would be absurd to demand from him ethical or political treatises, that which underlies his poetry and lends it a measure of solidity is often something ethical, metaphysical, or political. The work of Spenser which aims highest and opens the profoundest questions, is beyond doubt the fragment on Mutability; and where would that be without the philosophy that informs it? His lovely *Hymns*, perhaps his most perfect work, are nothing but Plato, as the *Faerie Queene* itself is largely Aristotle; and it is safe to say that Spenser's wandering genius is least erratic when his eye is on the *Symposium* or the *Ethics*.

With Shelley the case is the same. He is the most poetical of poets because he is, in the sense at which we have hinted, the most philosophical. His poems are often like additional "Myths" to illustrate the doctrines of Plato; and repeatedly his lighter lyrics, which otherwise might almost vanish in their gossamer tenuity, gain an element of permanence from an underlying stratum of philosophy. Take for example the exquisite verses entitled *The Invitation*, beginning "Best and brightest, come away." This poem, as light and dainty as if it had been sent by Herrick to Julia, is yet saved from mere prettiness by its undertone of something

deeper, which actually breaks into expression in the
last two lines:

> And all things seem only one
> In the universal sun.

Here the reference to the One and the Many—the
problem of harmonising which is the subject of so many
works with which Shelley was familiar, from the
Timaeus of Plato to the *Ethics* of Spinoza—is as plain
as it is in the famous fifty-second stanza of *Adonais*; but
the poetry is only the more beautiful because of the
philosophy. For, as we re-read it in the light of that
last couplet, we see how the idea was sub-consciously
present to Shelley's mind throughout, and how he
regarded the union of his heart with that of Jane
Williams as but a shadow of the unity of all things in
the Eternal. And this poem, again, gives some indication
of the limits beyond which philosophy should *not* be
driven in poetry. It should be present, but not obtrusive;
its voice should be still and small; in the words which
Charles II used of Sidney Godolphin, it should never
be in the way and never out of the way. Through the
neglect of one half of this principle many of the
speeches which Milton assigns to the Father fall under
the deserved censure of Pope; while on the other hand
those hymns, so terribly common in our service-books,
which have no substratum of theological thought at all,
"have not vitality enough to preserve them from
putrefaction."

All this is well illustrated in the stanza which we
propose briefly to study in this paper—the forty-third

of *Adonais*. In it we shall find touches of philosophy—
but the philosophy will not always be self-consistent;
and moving poetry, but poetry which has to be understood as well as felt:

> He is a portion of the loveliness
> Which once he made more lovely: he doth bear
> His part, while the One Spirit's plastic stress
> Sweeps through the dull dense world, compelling there
> All new successions to the forms they wear;
> Torturing the unwilling dross, which checks its flight,
> To its own likeness, as each mass may bear;
> And bursting, in its beauty and its might,
> From trees and beasts and men into the heaven's light.

In the first line the philosophy is that of the *Phaedrus*
and the *Symposium*, in which the essential unity is said
to be Love or Beauty—the eldest as well as the youngest
of the gods, the chiefest author and giver of virtue in
life and of happiness after death, the Pattern to whose
perfect mould the Creator has fashioned all things. This
"awful Loveliness," as Shelley calls it in his *Hymn to
Intellectual Beauty*, is but one, but it manifests itself in
myriad forms, and one of those forms was the spirit
that dwelt in Adonais. While it dwelt in him, it expressed
itself in concrete images of beauty, and may thus be
said to have made itself more lovely than it was before.
But the transient form must be withdrawn into the
eternal essence; Adonais is taken back into the loveliness of which he was but one manifestation. Elsewhere
this truth is put differently. In Mr Archer Hind's
Introduction to the Timaeus, Plato's view is thus given:
"The material universe is, as it were, a luminous

symbol-embroidered veil which hangs for ever between
finite existences and the Infinite, as a consequence of
the evolution of one out of the other. And none but the
highest of finite intelligences may lift a corner of this
veil and behold aught that is behind it." This is perhaps
Shelley's favourite image; he uses it at least four times.
"Lift not the painted veil which those who live call
life," he says in one of his *Sonnets*, and twice does he
repeat the warning in the *Prometheus*, as well as once
in his prose fragment on Life. On that veil Adonais
has painted beautiful shapes; and, though they are
"unreal," as Shelley tells us in the sonnet, they yet
add to the beauty of the great Whole from which they
spring and into which they are to pass. To use the
imagery of a later stanza, Keats's life may have stained
the white radiance of Eternity, but the stains, while
they last, are more beautiful than the whiteness.

But, almost in the same breath, Shelley leaves behind
him the idea of beauty as one of the attributes of the
Eternal, and substitutes for it another which, if less
consonant, perhaps, with the general thought of Plato,
is none the less Platonic, and is certainly more in
harmony with Shelley's own usual form of speech—
that, in fact, of a Spirit in effort. This Spirit is not
personal—*i.e.* Shelley would not, in plain prose, have
called it so—but it lends itself easily to Shelley's
favourite figure of personification—that figure which is
the life of all his poetry. The Spirit is One, and it is ever
striving after an end or purpose. This is Plato's Telos,
that divine event to which the whole creation moves;

the Idea in the mind of the Demiurgus when he made
the world. The Spirit is a *moulding* Spirit, like that
Eros which, in a well-known epigram of Meleager,
moulded Heliodora, the soul of his soul, within his
heart. For the actual expressions used we must probably seek an origin outside of Plato. Medieval science
imagined a plastic force in the earth[1], by virtue of
which she "moulded" inorganic substances into vital
and organic forms; and it was this theory which modern
geology had to destroy before it could make any advance.
To it Sir Thomas Browne alludes in the *Garden of
Cyrus*, when he speaks of the "plastical principle" as
not only inherent in the earth as a whole, but lodged
in the most diminutive of seeds. And Lord Herbert
of Cherbury, in his Latin poem entitled *Vita* (*Auto-
biography*, p. 17), speaks of the "plastica virtus" which
animated the first substance, and sent its juices through

---

[1] Thus, according to Lyell (*Principles of Geology*, 10th edn., I. 20), Theophrastus,
treating of ivory and bones, "supposed them to be produced by a certain plastic virtue
latent in our earth," and on p. 40 we are told that Dr Plot (1677) in his *Natural History
of Oxfordshire* still held the view of Theophrastus.

It may be worth while noticing that the LXX version of Genesis ii. 7 runs as follows:
"God *moulded* (ἔπλασε) man of the dust (χοῦν) of the ground, and breathed into
his face (εἰς τὸ πρόσωπον) breath of life; and placed in Eden the man whom he
had *moulded*."

Now on this passage Philo, a zealous student of the *Timaeus*, comments as follows
(Kennedy, *Philo's Contribution to Religion*, p. 76): "Most clearly does he show by
this that there is an immense difference between the man now formed (πλασθέντος)
and him who had earlier come into being (γεγονότος) according to the image of God
(Gen. i. 27). For the man now formed was perceptible by sense, already participating
in quality, composed of body and soul, man or woman, mortal by nature; while he
who was made after the Divine image was a sort of idea or class or soul, apprehensible
only by thought, incorporeal, neither male nor female, immortal by nature. More-
over, he says that the constitution of the individual man, perceptible by sense, was
composed of earthly substance and the Divine breath. For what he breathed into him
was nothing else than a Divine breath which took its departure hither from that
blessed and happy nature for the good of our race. So that if it is mortal so far as its
visible part is concerned, as regards its invisible part at least it possesses immortality."

It will be seen from this passage how differently two disciples of Plato, like Shelley
and Philo, can make their deductions from their master's doctrines: and yet how
essentially at one they are despite their superficial divergence.

the whole mass, precisely as man is formed in embryo. Even two poets so opposite as Charles Wesley and Matthew Prior availed themselves, each in his characteristic fashion, of this idea. "You know," says Prior in *Alma*,

> You know a certain lady, Dick,
> Who saw me when I last was sick;
> She kindly talked, at least three hours,
> Of plastic forms and mental powers.

Wesley's allusion is, as might be expected, more spiritual in tone and more theistic in sentiment:

> Thou art the universal soul,
> The plastic power that rules the whole,
>   And governs earth, air, sea, and sky;
> The creatures all thy breath receive,
> And who by thy inspiring live
>   Without thy inspiration die.

But there can be little doubt that, consciously or unconsciously, Shelley's phraseology was suggested by the last two lines of Coleridge's Sonnet to Bowles, which was published in 1796 in a volume of "Poems":

> As the great Spirit erst with plastic sweep
> Moved on the darkness of the unformed deep,

in which the medieval doctrine of a mysterious Power is blended with that of the Mosaic cosmogony.

The One Spirit, whose "plastic stress" thus moves the world, is the Universal Soul of the Platonists and Neo-Platonists—the soul from which all souls derive, and to which they return. This idea undoubtedly came to the Neo-Platonists from the ἡ τοῦ παντὸς ψυχή

(Soul of the All) of the *Timaeus* (41 D), a dialogue on
which Porphyry is said to have written a commentary,
and which, by its allegorical strain no less than by its
general tone of thought, naturally attracted his attention, as it had attracted that of his master Plotinus. We
give here a translation of the relevant chapter of the
Timaeus:

Into the same bowl wherein he (the divine Artificer)
mingled and blended the universal soul, he poured what was
left of the former, mingling it after the same manner, yet
no longer so pure as before, but second and third in pureness.
And when he had compounded the whole he portioned off
souls equal in number to the stars, and distributed a soul
to each star, and setting them in the stars as though in a
chariot, he showed them the nature of the universe and
declared to them its fated laws. . . . And should they master
their passions they would live in righteousness; if otherwise, in unrighteousness. And he who lived well throughout
his allotted time should be conveyed once more to a habita-
tion in his kindred star, and there should enjoy a blissful
and congenial life.

That Shelley was thinking of this passage must be
obvious to the most cursory reader of stanza 46, where
we learn that the soul of Adonais *has* returned to the
star of its kinship:

"Thou art become as one of us," they cry.
"It was for thee yon kingless sphere has long
Swung blind in unascended majesty,
Silent, alone, amid a heaven of song:
Assume thy winged throne, thou Vesper of our throng."

Like the Aster of Plato's epigram, he has become
Hesperus, "giving new splendour to the dead"; and

his soul, as we are told in the last stanza of the poem, is as a star, beaconing from the abode of the eternal.

We notice here that Shelley has discarded the notion of the Artificer or Demiurgus, and treats the Universal Soul as—for poetical purposes—the ultimate and "personal" original of all things. But the Universal Soul, no more than the Demiurgus, can work without hindrance. It finds the "world" in which it energises "dull and dense." Here Shelley has mingled with Plato's later theories some of his earlier, which he held in common with certain of his predecessors and successors, but rejected later, as to the intractability and "reality" of matter. As Plato developed his philosophy, he seems to have reached at length an idealism as uncompromising as that of Berkeley himself. The best interpreters of the *Theaetetus*, the *Timaeus*, and the *Philebus*, for example, tell us that in these dialogues "matter" becomes only a name for the perceptions of the finite soul: apart from the percipient it has no existence whatever. Soul is the sum-total of existence, and all, therefore, that exists independently of the finite soul is the Universal Soul, and even that includes the finite souls within itself, as the ultimate unity includes plurality. This view is probably that which commended itself to Shelley the *philosopher*—or rather he may have preferred to adopt the symbolism of Spinoza, and to call Matter and Thought parallel or coequal aspects of the same divine essence. But Shelley the *poet* was under no obligation to hold such a belief exclusively or even to hold that Plato held it. In him there was room for other theories at the same time; and accordingly in these lines we find matter to be the clogging, impeding vesture of decay that hinders the full expression of the One Spirit. As the Spirit obtains more and more control over Matter, so, to use Spenser's setting of Plato's view as given in the *Symposium*,

> So it more faire accordingly it makes,
> And the grosse matter of this earthly myne
> Which clotheth it thereafter doth refyne,
> Doing away the drosse which dims the light
> Of that faire beame which therein is empyght:

but it is a slow and weary business, and is not accomplished even at the "death" of the finite soul; nay, if we are allowed to personify, we may say that the One Spirit is glad of all the help it can get from finite souls in performing this tedious task. If they "bear their part" well, the thing will be done sooner.

But all this time, however rambling Shelley may be, he keeps his eye on the *Timaeus*, in which this process is described somewhat differently. We there learn that as the Spirit works upon "matter," matter receives determination, and expresses itself in "form": in these forms Plato finds the ultimate causes of the differences in our sensuous perceptions of things. This idea is more fully worked out in the system of Plotinus—a writer in whom, as in Plato and Spinoza, Shelley found congenial food both for his reasoning and for his imaginative powers. Here, however, there is a difference, of which traces may be found in the *Adonais*: in Plotinus the absolute and unconditioned One is regarded not as Spirit but as something still higher, from which in fact

Spirit is a kind of emanation. It is in Spirit, says Plotinus, that we first find the germ of plurality, and a basis alike for Thinking and for Being. Pursuing Spirit—in a manner similar to that of Spinoza in his *Ethics*—along the line of Being, we arrive finally at Matter, the lowest and meanest of all principles; in itself a negation, and so far a pure evil. Nevertheless, "inasmuch as it admits of Form," says Plotinus, it cannot be entirely negative and evil; it must contain an element of the positive and good, and admits, so far as this element exists, of being translated into a higher sphere of Being.

Here then we see the origin of Shelley's phrase,

> Compelling there
> All new successions to the forms they wear;

but we must not omit to notice that he has not bound himself to any single philosophy; "nullius addictus," he preserves a Horatian independence. So far as he conceives the ultimate Principle as Spirit, he is Platonic; in his doctrine of Forms, though doubtless he could have found some authority in Plato, he appears rather as Plotinian.

That the Artificer constrains all things to his own likeness is a conception well known, not merely in the difficult allegory of the *Timaeus*, but in the more concrete language of Milton and Spenser. "The Creator from his work desisting," says Milton, returned to his high abode,

> Thence to behold this new-created world,
> The addition of his empire, how it showed,
> Answering his great Idea.

So in the *Hymn in Honour of Beautie*, Spenser tells us,

> What time this World's great Work-Maister did cast
> To make all things such as we now behold,
> It seems that he before his eyes had plast
> A goodly Paterne, to whose perfect mould
> He fashioned them as comely as he could,
> That now so faire and seemely they appeare,
> As nought may be amended any where.

"The work of the artificer who looks always to the abiding and the unchangeable," says Plato, "and who designs and fashions his work after an unchangeable pattern, must of necessity be made fair and perfect. . . . If the world be indeed fair and the artificer good, then, as is plain, he must have looked to that which is eternal. . . . *And likening it to the All* he shaped it like a sphere and assigned it to the intelligence of the supreme to follow after it; and he disposed it throughout all the firmament of heaven, to be an adornment of it in very truth. In this way then and for this cause were created all such of the stars as wander through the heavens and turn about therein, in order that this universe may be most like to the perfect and ideal animal by its assimilation to the eternal being" (*Timaeus*, 39 E).

Matter, thus energised by the eternal Spirit, works its way upwards, as we have seen that it has the power of doing, from the inorganic to the organic, from the organic to the plant-kingdom, and so through beasts and men back to God from whom it came. The hint for this is found in the same passage of the *Timaeus* (40 A), where we learn that "so many forms as Mind perceived to exist in the ideal animal, according to their variety and multitude, such kinds and such a number did he think fit that this universe should possess"; and later (42 A) we are told that of all living creatures man is the highest as the most "god-fearing." All these, it is true, are but phantoms; as Shelley informs us in *Hellas*, this whole

> Of suns and worlds, and men, and beasts, and flowers,
> With all the silent or tempestuous workings
> By which they have been, are, or cease to be,
> Is but a vision;—all that it inherits
> Are motes of a sick eye, bubbles and dreams.
> Thought is its cradle and its grave; nor less
> The future and the past are idle shadows
> Of Thought's eternal flight;—they have no being;
> Nought is but that which feels itself to be:

yet they are capable of *putting on* being as the eternal works in them; as they "look on that which cannot change, the One, the unborn, and the undying"; as Ficino says, "*cupiditas perfectionis proprie propagandae amor quidam est.*" The final symbolic expression of the ultimate perfection as "heaven's light" is almost too obvious and too common to need illustration. Shelley, assuredly, who was convinced that "men scarcely know how beautiful fire is," had no need to seek outside of his own mind for this type of the One Spirit, or of the Beauty wherein all things work and move, or of the all-sustaining Love, or of whatever else he chose to call the Absolute. He might have thought of Spenser's lines, borrowed as they are from Plato and Ficino:

> Man, having yet in his deducted spright
> Some sparks remaining of that *heavenly fyre*,
> He is enlumind with that *goodly light*,
> Unto like goodly semblant to aspyre:

> For sure, of all that in this mortall frame
> Contained is, nought more divine doth seeme,
> Or that resembleth more th' immortal flame
> Of heavenly light, then Beauties glorious beame.

But in this symbolism the daring unbeliever Shelley is at one with the beloved disciple John—to both alike God is light, and in him is no darkness at all.

It remains to consider briefly what is the plain prose of this poetic philosophy. It is unnecessary to adduce Shelley's own expressions as to the immortality of the soul—they are collected in Rossetti's edition of *Adonais*, and indeed may easily be found by anyone who likes to glance through the prose writings. But while those passages prove conclusively that Shelley had no belief in the ordinary doctrine of immortality, they yet leave us in doubt as to the *kind* of immortality which he expected for Keats, and which, in poetical symbolism, he asserts for him in this poem. For, while he allowed himself the utmost license of figurative language, and could scarcely touch an abstraction without personifying it, he yet was incapable of saying in his poetry a single word in which he did not believe. Sincerity was the very breath of his nostrils. And, as Rossetti has omitted to discuss this point (just as he has given but the shortest of notes to the whole stanza we have been discussing), we think it desirable briefly to consider the question.

First, there can be small doubt that Shelley understood the real meaning of the allegorical language of Plato. He knew, for example, that the assignment of souls to stars meant simply the innate difference of character in individuals: Plato meant not much more than our ancestors meant when they assigned to a jovial person a close connection with Jupiter, or to a mercurial person a dependence on Mercury. When then Shelley tells us that *Adonais* is taking his proper place in a heaven of *song*, he simply indicates that Keats has already, in the judgment of his peers, taken his true rank among poets: his *Hyperion* has placed him beside, if below, Milton. He is indeed "robed in the dazzling immortality" which belongs alike to those whose names are remembered and to those whose names are forgotten though their influence lives; but it is the immortality of the work, not of the man. He has made loveliness more lovely by his additions to our store of Beauty—and that beauty is a joy for ever: but Keats the person is dead.

Again, Shelley was neither ignorant nor careless of the difference between the Immortal and the Eternal. An amoeba may be considered immortal: it is so low in the scale of being as not to have attained to the privilege of death; but the Eternal is outside of time altogether. No one had insisted more emphatically on this distinction than Shelley's favourite Spinoza, the whole of whose *Ethics* is indeed based on that difference. Now in the famous fifth part of the *Ethics* perhaps the most famous proposition is the twenty-third: "Mens humana non potest cum corpore absolute destrui, sed ejus aliquid remanet quod aeternum est." "The human mind cannot utterly perish with the body, but something

of it remains that is eternal." This statement has often
been taken as an assertion of the immortality of the
soul; but Shelley was not likely to view it in this light.
He knew too well the meaning of Spinoza's phrase *sub
specie aeternitatis*. The properties of a triangle, for
instance, are eternal when they are deducible from its
essence, and are not the accidental properties of any
particular triangle. Similarly, the eternity of the mind
of man denotes, not the survival of the soul after death,
but the "adequacy" of his ideas. Eternity is not to
be found in the future, but here and now; it is not
open to all, but in the strict sense only to the possessors
of these adequate ideas, and the way to attain it is to
increase our stock of such ideas. Let a man make a
real addition to our store, and *so far* he is immortal;
these ideas, being seen *sub specie aeternitatis*, can never
die.

Now to Shelley, if not perhaps to Spinoza, the idea
of Beauty is as "adequate" as any to be obtained in
mathematics itself. It is eternal: and no man had done
more than Keats to enlarge our perceptions of it. "Something of the mind of Keats then remained that was
eternal": the thoughts he had given us were taken up
into the thought of God, and lasted when the body died.
But it was no *personal* survival; personality to Shelley,
as to Spinoza, was a sub-illusion of the great deception,
Time. Hence to say that Adonais "bears his part" in
the work of the One Spirit is not to say that he is
consciously working: he has contributed his *aliquid*,
which can never now be subtracted from the great

sum; but he is absorbed into the whole, and can no longer, even in imagination, be conceived apart from it. New "successions" will take his place; the changing Many will pass endlessly on in its phantom army, for ever appearing, and for ever falling back into the One: but he, as we knew him, will awake no more, ah, nevermore!

But there is yet one thing left to be considered. Shelley may have regarded Matter, with Plato, as non-existent except in the mind of its percipient; and he may, with Spinoza, have viewed the individual as a mere phantom. He would probably have endorsed every word of the statement of Mr F. H. Bradley: "Every kind of process between the Many is a state of the Whole in and through which the Many subsist. The process of the Many, and the total being of the Many themselves, are mere aspects of the one Reality which moves and knows itself within them, and apart from which all things and their changes, and every knower and every known, is absolutely nothing." But—and here is the really important part of Shelley's doctrine—he held, as strongly as Plato himself, that the "process of the Many" is an *advance*, and an advance toward good. All finite things are imperfect, but they are tending to something higher; and ultimately—in time or out of it—they make an asymptotic approach to it. Absorption in the One, then, is not a mere suppression of the individual; it is its assumption into that after which it strives, and an attainment of, or a step towards, its ideal. For Adonais to become a portion of Loveliness is no annihilation; any more than for Goethe it was annihilation to find the Light for which he longed. To a poet the "heaven of song" may not be the heaven of popular thought, but it is a heaven nevertheless: and Keats, who feared that his name had been writ in water, would have been well content could he have been assured that he would gain that heaven.

IX

Macaulay's Lay Figures

Palatinus sighed
Faint echoes of Ionian song.
SHELLEY.

THE care and accuracy which distinguish the *Lays of Ancient Rome*, as they distinguish everything that Macaulay wrote, are almost a proverb. Thus, for example, when he decided to alter

> By heaven, he said, yon rebels
> > Stand manfully at bay,

into

> Quoth he, The she-wolf's litter
> > Stand savagely at bay,

he notes that "litter" is used by our best writers as governing the plural number (Trevelyan's *Life*, p. 413)[1]. And again, in November 1839, when he was at Rome, he went towards the river, to the spot where the old Pons Sublicius stood. "I looked about," he tells us, "to see how my Horatius agreed with the topography. Pretty well; but his house must be on Mount Palatine; for he would never see Mount Coelius from the spot where he fought" (Trevelyan, p. 359). Thus for the old

> But he saw upon Mount Coelius

we now read

> But he saw on Palatinus
> The white porch of his home.

When then Macaulay gives us a name for which actual authority is lacking, we expect, and we usually

---

[1] When no question of euphony arises, Macaulay makes "litter" take a singular. "The vile Claudian litter still yelps and snaps" (*Virginia*, 260).

find, just that touch of appropriateness which marks the scholar—an appropriateness more satisfying than the mere alliterative suitability of the "high-born Hoel" or the "mountain-mourned Modred" which we meet in Gray. Even the "tall Pinta" of the Armada is hardly an exception[1]: and genuine exceptions are rare. Of course Macaulay did not arrogate to himself the praise of an imaginative poet, nor do the *Lays* lend themselves to the highest flights of imagination.

> Tall are the oaks whose acorns
>   Drop in dark Auser's rill,

says he in *Horatius*. Shelley, describing the same rill in his *Boat on the Serchio*, tells us how the river,

>   twisting forth
> Between the marble barriers which it clove
> At Ripafratta, leads through the dead chasm
> The wave that died the death which lovers love,
>   Living in what it sought—

a touch beyond Macaulay's reach. Yet Macaulay has his own gifts. He is a master of that suggestiveness which is so distinct a feature of Milton, of Virgil, and (in a lesser degree) of Scott. Like them, he loves the proper name not merely for its sound but for its associations, and the associations generally add much to the power and penetration of his lines. Who, for instance, on reading the couplet from the *Epitaph on a Jacobite*,

> Heard on Lavernia Scargill's whispering trees,
> And pined by Arno for my lovelier Tees,

can fail to perceive the subtle allusiveness which turns topography itself into music? And over and over again

[1] There was a "Pinta" among the ships of Columbus, though not in the Armada.

we light on some suggestion, some underlying reference, that we may have previously missed, and then we experience the same sort of pleasure as when we discover that a beautiful line of Gray or Tennyson, full of meaning as it was before, is yet fuller when seen to be a reminiscence from some classical author.

The *Lays of Ancient Rome* are indeed crowded with such touches. Whether they are "trifles" or not, not only are they, in the words of Macaulay's favourite Johnson, "a model in the art of writing trifles with dignity" (Trevelyan, p. 664), but they do at least, as Macaulay put it in a letter to Macvey Napier (July 14, 1842), "pass for scholarly and not inelegant trifles." They were on his hands for fully six years, and he began to mark his Livy with a view to them while he was still in India. Thus, if they have not the highest signs of genius, they abound in beauties of suggestion. The roll of names at the beginning of *Horatius*, for example, has a charm of this kind[1]. We know of course that Macaulay drew the inspiration for it from an actual journey through Tuscany; and his sister believed she could tell the very turn of the road where the words struck him,

> From where Cortona lifts to heaven
> Her diadem of towers[2],

[1] Macaulay thought his *Fragments of a Roman Tale* showed sadly unripe scholarship (T. 666); but within their range they are marked by the same qualities as *Horatius*.
[2] There can, I think, be little doubt that both the sound and the sense of this line were suggested by Dante's words (*Inferno*, xxxi. 41):

> Montereggion di torri si corona;

Cortona reminding him of *corona*. This does not imply that Macaulay's mind did not run on to the innumerable classical parallels—*e.g. Hecuba*, 910:

> ἀπὸ δὲ στεφάναν κέκαρσαι
> πύργων—

"Thou hast been shorn of thy coronal of towers."

but the aroma, the poetry, is in the sound and in the recollected romance behind the names. "Lordly Vola-terrae," "sea-girt Populonia," "Massilia's triremes," these words derive their glamour from a history.

The same, in a sense, is true even of the invented names of persons whose business it is to carry on the story. It is interesting merely to guess at the line of thought that suggested these names to Macaulay; precisely as there is an interest in tracing the old ballad or romance that gave to Rossetti one of the "stunning words" which lend their glamour to *Sister Helen* or the *White Ship*. Sometimes, it is true, Macaulay himself must have been hard put to it to know the exact impulse that dictated the choice. Verbenna, for instance, is doubtless born of the sound: it is apparently Etruscan, and will therefore "do"[1]; and in *Regillus* there are many such names. It is perhaps scarcely worth noting that a Flaccus, a Julius[2], and a Nepos are all mentioned in a single line of Martial (x. 48, 5); nor does there seem to be more than a Latin origin in common between Cicero's friend and relative Tubero, the accuser of Ligarius (*Pro Ligario*, 1), and the Tubero of Norba whom Aebutius gave to feed the Porcian kites. Metius, again, with his long fair curls, bears slight likeness to Metius Fufetius, the treacherous king of Alba, to whom Tullus Hostilius dealt out such dire punishment, or to

[1] The Etruscans, it is said, called themselves Rasena; and the well-known Sisenna is perhaps an Etruscan name.

[2] Why one of the Julian line should devote himself to Tarquin is hard to see; we should have rather expected to find him among the denouncers of Claudius in Virginia. But his mansion was on the Velian Hill because the Aedes Penatium, so closely associated with Iulus, stood there. In this shrine were preserved the old Trojan household gods.

Metius Curtius, whose famous leap is said to have
given a name to the Curtian Lake.

But other names, unquestionably, are meant to rouse
definite associations in our minds. Capys, the sightless
seer, recalls the Capys of Virgil, whose mind had formed
a sound opinion, and whose advice was to destroy the
fatal horse. He recalls also (if this be not the same man)
that Capys from whom the name of the Campanian
city is derived (*Aen.* x. 145), a follower specially dear
to Aeneas.

Horatius, indeed, is crowded with such names.
Tolumnius with the belt of gold is meant to remind us
first of that augur in Virgil (xii. 460):

> Primus in adversos telum qui torserat hostes,

and secondly of that Etruscan king whose "spolia
opima," perhaps with a gilded belt among them, were
carried off in triumph by Cossus and affixed to the walls
of the temple of Jupiter (Livy, iv. 19). Incidentally,
we may hazard the conjecture that this same Cossus
sat for the portrait of the keen-sighted horseman whom
at a crisis of the Regillus battle the Dictator sent with
a message to Herminius. Astur, the great Lord of
Luna, plainly comes from the tenth book of the *Aeneid*
(180), where we read

> sequitur pulcherrimus Astur,
> Astur equo fidens et versicoloribus armis;

nor is his by any means the only name conveyed from
the well-known passage (x. 163 *sq.*) in which Virgil
enumerates the Tuscan chiefs who came to the help of

Aeneas. This book, indeed, must have appealed specially
to Macaulay. "I like Virgil best," he wrote to his friend
Ellis, "on Italian ground. I like his localities; his
national enthusiasm; his frequent allusions to his
country, its history, its antiquities, and its greatness.
In this respect he often reminds me of Sir Walter Scott,
with whom, in the general character of his mind, he
had very little affinity" (Trevelyan, p. 169). It was, in
fact, in the Virgil of the later books that Macaulay
found unconsciously some image of himself; and the
tenth book, in particular, supplied him with many
touches for his *Lays*. "The Laurentian jungle, the wild
hog's reedy home," comes straight from the passage
(x. 709) where Virgil compares Mezentius to the wild
boar

> Long fostered in Laurentum's fen
> Mid reeds and marshy ground.

The very similar passage in *Horatius* (stanza 39) also
reminds us, as it obviously reminded Conington when
translating Virgil, of the same book. The city of Cosa,
an obscure little place where dwelt the wild boar slain
by Aruns, is mentioned by Virgil in close connection
with Clusium; and half-a-dozen lines farther down we
find Populonia, Pisae, and Ilva or Elba,

> Insula inexhaustis Chalybum generosa metallis—

Elba rich in iron mines. Ocnus of Falerii recalls the
Ocnus on whom Virgil lingers with patriotic pride, the
son of the Tuscan river and of Manto, and the founder
of Mantua, "whose strength is of Tuscan blood."

Aunus of Tifernum, again, though the tenth book knows nothing of such a name, reminds us of that dweller on the Apennine mentioned in the eleventh, whose crafty Ligurian son did not escape the vengeance of Camilla by all his wiles (l. 700).

Others of Macaulay's names reveal a different origin. Seius, for instance, "whose eight hundred slaves sicken in Ilva's mines," may possibly be nothing but a John Doe or Richard Roe, for the name constantly occurs thus in Roman law-books, but it is far more probably meant to refer us to Seius Strabo, the father of the infamous Sejanus. It would not have been necessary for Macaulay to turn up his Tacitus in order to recall the fact that Sejanus was of Tuscan extraction, and born close by that Volsinian mere of which we have already heard; indeed he could scarcely look at the lake without thinking of the enigmatic villain whose birth-place was so near. Cruelty to slaves, and a mad avarice, might well be attributed to the ancestor of such a man. Nor must we forget that in the passage of Juvenal which describes the fall of Sejanus—a passage which Macaulay assuredly knew by heart—the Volsinian goddess Nurtia is mentioned; and thus, when he wrote the lines

> And hang round Nursia's altars
> The golden shields of Rome,

his thoughts must have travelled to Sejanus (Juv. x. 74).

Another imperial favourite, more deserving than Sejanus, supplied Macaulay with another name. Gaius Cilnius Maecenas, it is well known, claimed truly or falsely to be descended from an old line of Etruscan kings of Arretium; and the poets who lived by his bounty never failed to celebrate the splendour of his ancestry and the contrasting simplicity of his life.

Maecenas, eques Etrusco de sanguine regum,

says Propertius; what Horace says there is no need to quote. We are not surprised, then, to find "Cilnius of Arretium" among the Lucumos that followed Porsena. Aruns, again, is a name occurring often in Etruscan annals; so often, indeed, that it has been regarded by some as a mere common noun, meaning younger son. Three of the name are found among the family of the Tarquins, whom "every schoolboy knows" to have been of Etruscan origin; and Livy mentions an Aruns who was a son of Lars Porsena himself. Lucan tells us of another who

Incoluit desertae moenia Lunae (I. 586).

No wonder that legend gave the name to the Clusine traitor who invited Brennus and his Gauls to invade Tuscany, or that Virgil pictures an Aruns as the cowardly slayer of the Amazon Camilla. Lausulus of Urgo and Picus of Umbria are difficult. Lausulus one might guess to be a relative of Lausus the son of the tyrant Mezentius, taking, however, rather after the latter than after the former. His death—"Lie there, fell pirate"—is obviously modelled on that of Tarquitus in Virgil (X. 557), "istic nunc metuende iaces." Picus may remind us of the eponymous ancestor of Picenum, the country that borders on Umbria—perhaps the "Picus, equum domitor" of *Aen.* VII. 189. It may be worth mentioning that Picus was the father of Faunus, and Faunus of Tarquitus: it is thus easy to see how Macaulay's thought advanced from Picus to the death of Lausulus.

In *Regillus*, as we have already hinted, there is less to detain us than in *Horatius*; the main interest of the literary detective in the former poem is to trace the reminiscences of Homer rather than those of Livy or Virgil. Yet there is something to reward our search even here. A Caeso or Kaeso among the Fabii is what we should expect to find. One of the many Kaesos of that family was the leader of the three hundred and six Fabii who held the fortress of the Cremera so gloriously against Veii, and perished with the exception of a single boy; a tale, by the way, on which Macaulay dwells at length in his preface. Rex of Gabii[1], again, refers us to the kingly office of the priest. We may compare the well-known Rex sacrificulus of Rome, or the Rex nemorensis of Nemi, to whom Macaulay himself refers in the characteristically exact lines:

> Aricia's trees,
> Those trees in whose dim shadow
> The ghastly priest doth reign,
> The priest who slew the slayer,
> And shall himself be slain.

Tullus of Arpinum (stanza 36), also, is obviously an ancestor of Marcus Tullius Cicero, the great glory of that little town. Not far from Arpinum was the legendary home of Tullus Hostilius.

---

[1] For Juno's shrine cp. *Aen.* VII. 682, and other passages.

Black Auster[1], the famous steed of Herminius, is of
course named from the south-west wind—a natural
name for a horse: but is it impossible that Macaulay
was thinking of Aquilo (north wind), the ancient
Eclipse which won the first prize a hundred and thirty
times, and whose grandson Hirpinus was equally successful? (Martial III. 63; Juvenal VIII. 63; see Prof.
Mayor's note).

Matthew Arnold, it will be remembered, in his anxiety
to score a point over Frank Newman, called the *Lays*
"pinchbeck ballads." Like most ballads, as we have
admitted, they fail to reach the height of imaginative
poetry: as Leigh Hunt told Macaulay himself in his
famous begging-letter, they want the aroma that
breathes from the *Faerie Queene*. Their moving impulse
was perhaps political rather than ethereal. Proud
Tarquin was to him a sort of James the Second; Valerius
an earlier Schomberg; Titus was the Duke of Berwick;
Julius was Sarsfield, and Regillus a luckier Steinkirk:
nay, the Sublician Bridge was the bridge over the
Gette, which William, retreating before Luxemburg,
crossed so unwillingly[2]. Had there been no British
significance in these old Roman stories, nay, had they
not possessed a specially Whig significance, Macaulay
would never have retold them with such spirit. But
though his inspiration thus came as much from Constitu-

[1] Nigerrimus Auster, *Georgics* III. 278.
[2] "The enemy pressed on him so close that it was with difficulty that he at length
made his way over the Gette. A small body of brave men, who shared his peril to
the last, could hardly keep off the pursuers as he crossed the bridge." (*History*,
Chapter XX, describing Landen, 1693.) Who can doubt that Macaulay thought of
Horatius as he wrote these words? Nay, four or five lines below, he actually refers
to Horatius by name.

tion Hill as from Helicon, it is a high and genuine
inspiration nevertheless. Within their range, and considered from the point of view of their aim, the *Lays*
are not far from perfection. And if they be judged by
the skill with which, by an epithet, by a rhyme, by a
mere proper name, they call up trains of pleasing
associations, surely "pinchbeck" is the very last word
to use in order to characterise them. Long may it be
before the British people is too "superior" to enjoy
them!

X

Chaucer as a Critic of Dante

IN days like these, when so much that *has* happened is scarcely a subject for pleasant contemplation, it is a harmless amusement to picture to oneself what *might* have happened if things had been a little different. We have all spent time over such questions as "If Napoleon had won Waterloo," "If Hannibal had attacked Rome after Cannae," and the like. Similarly, in places where the current *Punch* was not to be had, we have found a good substitute in wondering what the *Rape of the Lock* would have been like if Milton had written it, or what sort of affair Bishop Butler would have made of *A Tale of a Tub*; nay, we have sometimes been so greatly daring as to speculate on the possible nature of a Don Juan written by Mrs Hannah More. This exercise, as the Dean of St Paul's says of prophesying, at any rate does no one any harm.

We have experienced a converse kind of pleasure when our thoughts, as they have sometimes done, have started automatically guessing the character of an *Excursion* by Sterne, or picturing the sort of *Divine Comedy* we might have had if Chaucer had taken Dante's theme in hand. There would have been less sublimity, fewer flights of high imagination, not so many purple patches, and, in general, less intensity, profundity, and power; but there would have been more geniality and more humour; nor are we sure that the result would not have been more satisfactory.

For example, had Chaucer gone a pilgrimage, not to Canterbury but to Hell, he would have shown a much greater human sympathy than Dante with the poor victims whom he met. Like Gunga Din, he would have thrown water on the flames, and would, when Virgil was not listening, have whispered that, after all, Hellgate was not so very well guarded, and that, despite appearances, there was perhaps a way out. The man who understood the hunting propensities of the Monk, and was not shocked by the vulgarities of the Miller or the embezzlements of the Manciple, would have found something consoling to say to a Nicholas the Third, and have made excuses for Boniface the Eighth himself. Nay, one may well suspect that he would have shown some of Tillotson's feeling even towards the great Author of Evil, and would have contrived to let us see that he is not so bad as he is painted. If Lucifer has done wrong he has suffered for it, and may in time obtain a remission of his sentence. Again, far from a democrat as Chaucer was, his wide and universal humanity would have found time for interviews not merely with the great but with the small; not merely with the Farinatas and the Montefeltros, but with the poor clerks, cooks, and tapicers whom Dante apparently despised too heartily even to damn them. In a word, a collaboration between Dante and Chaucer would have produced a Shakspere.

Poets are not always good critics; but there is a

peculiar interest in discovering what one poet thinks
of another. The judgment may be biassed, but it will,
at any rate, be well-informed. Nor is it always necessary
for the critic-poet to be a Coleridge or a Swinburne,
and to set down his opinions of his predecessors in
ordered form. We can tell what Tennyson thinks of
Virgil without reading his direct words on the subject:
his allusions, his imitations, and even some of his tricks
of style are sufficient evidence. It is thus that we should
be fully informed as to Gray's appreciation of Lucretius,
and as to Shelley's of Plato, Spenser's of Ariosto,
Morris's of Chaucer, even if no overt word of homage
were to be found in their works. And it is thus that
we know Chaucer's opinion of Dante. His was perhaps
the very first copy of the *Divine Comedy* ever brought
into England; and that he admired Dante, and admired
him even profoundly, must be obvious to every reader
of his poems. His Second Nun sings a hymn to the
Virgin, taken from the sublime cantica put by the
Florentine poet into the mouth of St Bernard (*Paradiso*,
XXXIII). He translated the story of Ugolino[1]. The only
terza rimas in English, till we come down to the time
of Wyatt, are Chaucer's. He actually names his great
predecessor four or five times, and he is constantly
quoting him without naming him. The commentators
enumerate forty or fifty passages in which Chaucer thus

---

[1] It is this translation, rather than the *House of Fame*, that we should regard as
the one referred to by Lydgate as *Dante in English* among the works of Chaucer. The
Tale of Ugolino bears all the marks of an independent exercise, which Chaucer by
an afterthought inserted among the Monk's tragedies. It is hard to think that even
Lydgate could call the *House of Fame* by so misleading a title. But of the actual relation of that poem to Dante we shall speak in the sequel.

draws upon the *Divine Comedy*: but their list is by no means exhaustive. For the references are often, though unmistakable, of the most subtle and elusive kind: as with Virgil's conveyings from Homer, they may be at times nothing more than the merest breath of fragrance, a turn of phrase, an alteration in the order of words. Not that the open pillage is rare. In *Troilus and Criseyde*, for instance, though the poem, of course, is based on Boccaccio, Chaucer seizes every opportunity of a theft from Dante. It is there that we find the famous passage, borrowed from the words of Francesca in the fifth canto of *Inferno*, and imitated in its turn by Tennyson:

> For of Fortunes sharpe adversitee
>   The worste kinde of infortune is this,
> A man to have been in prosperitee,
>   And hit remembren whanne hit passed is.

Here it is true Chaucer may be quoting less from Dante than from Boëthius, the ultimate original of all the retailers of the maxim: but when we notice that the second book of *Troilus* begins in similar language to the second part of the *Comedy*, that the poem ends with a verse taken straight from the *Paradiso*, and that some of the loveliest stanzas are Dante all over, doubt ends. It is, indeed, most interesting to notice the kind of beauty that Chaucer selects for imitation. From the famous passage in the second canto of *Inferno*:

> Quali i fioretti dal notturno gelo
> Chinati e chiusi, poiche il Sol gl' imbianca
> Si drizzan tutti aperti in loro stelo,

he borrows the lovely lines:

> But right as floures, thurgh the colde of nighte,
>   Yclosed, stoupen on hir stalkes lowe,
> Redressen hem ayein the sonne brighte,
>   And spreden on hir kinde cours by rowe:

from the *Purgatorio* (I. 20):

> Faceva tutto rider l'oriente,

he annexes (*Kn. Tale*, *A* 1494)

> That al the Orient laugheth of the lighte:

from *Inferno* (III. 19),

E poiche la sua mano alla mia pose,... ond' io mi confortai,

comes the line in the *Parlement of Foules*:

> With that my hand in his he took anon,
> Whereof I comfort caughte;

and we have no doubt that the favourite line, repeated so often in the *Canterbury Tales*:

> Pity renneth soone in gentil herte,

was suggested by *Inferno*, v. 100:

> Amor, che al cor gentil ratto s'apprende.

Nay, we are not sure that the imitation does not descend to the most trivial details, and that even Chaucer's rhymes of "to me" with "Rome," and the like, may not be due to Dante's "come" and "O me" (*Inferno*, XXVIII. 123, etc.). Anyone, in fact, who will but run through a Chaucer index, and note the kind of allusions made by the English poet to the Italian, will recognise that the "gran translateur" loved and admired certain aspects of the Florentine to the full, and paid his debts after the true fashion of a great poet, by continuing to borrow. His thefts, indeed, form a series of exquisite appreciations of Dante, as distinct, if not so elaborate, as those of a Church or a Ruskin.

Nor less interesting is it to note that his judgments are by no means always favourable. It was not possible for a man of Chaucer's kind to admire indiscriminately everything in Dante. The mental and moral natures of the two men were far too widely separated for such a result. We might have had an absolute panegyric from the author of *Piers the Plowman*; from the creator of Pandarus we can only expect to find admiration mingled with distaste: and this we get. Indeed, the total sum of Chaucer's criticism of Dante is at least as interesting from the light it throws on the critic as from that it throws on the criticised. And perhaps we may detect something of Chaucer's feeling from the very form into which his two greatest poems are cast. It is perhaps possible to take Chaucer's gradual disuse of the allegorical method as an implied criticism if not of Dante himself, yet of the style of which he is the most distinguished representative. Chaucer began in the approved fashion of his time, with allegories on the model of the *Romance of the Rose*. The *Parlement of Foules*, the *Complaint of Mars*, the prologue to the *Legend of Good Women* are all allegorical: nor did he drop the style when he passed from French to Italian models. But there were many reasons why a mind like Chaucer's should gradually discard it. Allegory is either obscure

or transparent. If it is obscure its meaning may be
utterly lost on its readers. Thus, in the two passages
where Dante tells us quite plainly that he is talking
allegory, every one of his commentators has a different
guess at his meaning, although in the one place Dante
says it only requires "intelletti sani," and in the other
he asserts that the veil is thin. But when the symbolism
really *is* transparent, it may well be that to a man like
Chaucer it might seem cheaper to do without it altogether. At any rate, in his best works he *does* dispense
with it, to the great advantage of his style and the delight
of his readers. After the *Legend* he neither wastes his
time on a symbolism that anyone can see through nor
seeks the reputation of profundity by a symbolism that
no one can penetrate[1].

But, after all, when Chaucer renounced allegory for
himself, it may well have been merely that he was
forming a right judgment of his own powers rather
than that he was consciously passing sentence on anyone else. Horace, declining to write epic, is appraising
Horace, not censuring Virgil. Similarly, when Chaucer,
who so closely resembles Horace on many sides of his
mind, drops the *Romance of the Rose* and takes to the
Canterbury Prologue, he need not have anyone but him-

---

[1] If anybody wishes to see how Chaucer could criticise one whom he intensely
admired, let him read the *Legend of Dido*. Here, after an exordium in which Virgil
receives a tribute that even he might well have been proud of, the English poet tells
the tale in such a way as to show clearly what he thought of the character of Aeneas
as drawn by Virgil in the Fourth Book. It is quite obvious that Chaucer saw and
appreciated the beauty of the most romantic episode in all Latin poetry; but it is
also obvious that he saw how fatally it ruins the whole remainder of the epic. Aeneas,
in fact, for Chaucer as for us to-day, had "done for himself," and nothing that Virgil
can do for him can make up for it.

self in mind. But—we whisper it with bated breath—
there is one defect in Dante, of a quite other kind from
that allegorising (if, indeed, that be a defect at all),
which must have forced itself on the keen senses of
his admirer. That total lack of humour, immense and
glaring, which is perhaps his only important weakness[1], none but the blindest and most undiscriminating
idolater can fail to see: and of all English poets Chaucer
would have been the first to feel it striking him in the
face.

He has a more than Wordsworthian insensibility to
incongruities, and passes direct from sublimity to
grotesqueness without a tremor. Among these incongruities we do not reckon the intrusion of classical myth
upon Christian verity: this was part of his time, and
need not disturb the student of the Middle Ages, nor the
lover of Milton and Spenser. But enough, and more
than enough, remain without it. The poet who can make
St Bernard, in the midst of a sublime theological discourse, talk of "cutting his coat according to his cloth,"
or who can interrupt his description of the four living
creatures by telling us that as to their wings he agrees
with St John, but differs from Ezekiel, must surely have
been utterly deficient in a sense of the incompatible.
When, after the glorious beginning of the *Paradiso*, we

---

[1] Readers of Morley's *Life of Gladstone* will remember the statesman's curious
reason for denying to Dante the very highest rank among poets—an excess of optimism:
an opinion very remarkable as coming from the most hopeful of politicians. It opens
a wide field for argument, and is well worthy of an article to itself: but it hardly falls
into place in the present discussion. It will be remembered that Lord Morley seems
astonished at Gladstone's view; but in his Introduction to the Globe *Wordsworth*
he adduces the same defect as a reason for refusing to Wordsworth the high pinnacle
to which he would otherwise have been entitled.

are suddenly plunged into a discussion as prosaic as a
treatise on Statics, we feel this defect still more. But
it is visible everywhere, and not least in the *Inferno*,
where, indeed, there is hardly a single circle that
has not something ludicrous, from Plutus, with his
clucking voice and "Pape Satan," to Lucifer, with
his three mouths grinding eternally at three kicking
traitors. As a result, it is doubtful if anyone was
ever really terrified by the horrors of the Dantesque
hell: indeed, we have known people who have fancied
that one of Dante's main motives in writing the
Inferno was similar to that of Lucretius, and that
he meant to cure the fear of future punishment by
a somewhat clumsy ridicule. A judge like Minos,
twisting his tail according to the number of circles the
sinner has to fall, is not dreadful, but merely absurd.
The picture of Geryon is almost worse: one has only
to *visualise* this combination of good man and dragon,
with claws, "nodi, rotelle," in order to see that this
"painted devil" could hardly frighten "the eye of childhood." As for Nimrod and the giants, they are no more
terrific than those overcome by Jack the Giant-Killer.
And when, as people without humour so often do,
Dante makes a desperate attempt to be really amusing
he is worst of all. The Barrators and their tormentors,
even if with Rossetti we believe them to be caricatures
of actual Florentine "grafters," remain the clumsiest
and most ludicrous bit of would-be satire ever essayed
by a great writer—and we are not forgetting the jests
of Belial. It is passages like these that all but justify

the criticism once passed on the *Inferno*, that the real parallel to it is not *Paradise Lost* or the *Pilgrim's Progress*, but *Gulliver's Travels*—and that *manqué*. But neither *Purgatorio* nor *Paradiso* is without similar grotesquenesses. The Griffin, whatever Dante's times may have thought of it, is a most pitiful symbol of the dual nature of Christ; and a Holy Rose, with ecclesiastics hiding in its petals, is scarcely better. One longs to syringe these parsons out.

All this, of course, must have been at least as visible to Chaucer as to us. We are not ignorant of the vigorous defence made by Ruskin and others against this charge; and we know well that there is an eleventh Bolgia prepared for those who make it. Dante's grotesque, says Ruskin, was the true kind, as some of the later Stones of Venice are the false kind: and, in fact, all questions as to poetic dignity are irrelevant in his case; he was above them. If then we are to be condemned to the lowest circle of Blasphemers against the Majesty of Alighieri, it is some comfort to think that in all probability Chaucer is there already. For that he perceived the weakness that went with Dante's intense earnestness and amazing strength not only is almost certain from his character and ways of thought, but may, we think, be demonstrated by concrete examples from his actual writings.

For instance, in the *House of Fame*, when Chaucer figures himself as carried off by the eagle to somewhat uncomfortable heights, we can scarcely doubt that he is making fun of that passage in the *Purgatorio* (IX. 22)

where Dante tells us of a dream in which he is rapt
aloft by a similar bird:

> Ed esser mi parea là dove foro
> Abbandonati i suoi da Ganimede.

This passage is serious enough; but Chaucer's ridicule
is exquisite:

> O God, thought I, that madest kynde,
> Shal I non other weyes dye?
> Wher Ioves wol me stellifye,
> Or what thing may this signifye?
> I neither am Enok ne Elye,
> Ne Romulus ne Ganymede,
> That was ybore up, as men rede,
> To heven with Dan Iupiter,
> And made the goddes boteler—
>
> *(House of Fame*, 584 *sqq.)*

in which we have not only a parody of the *Purgatorio*
dream, but also a sly stroke at Dante's hesitation before
accepting the guidance of Virgil in Hell:

> Io non Enea, io non Paolo sono.

Similarly, it can hardly be doubted that there is a grain
of malice in Chaucer's ascription to the eagle (*H. F.* 729)
of a lecture much of which is based upon a learned discourse uttered by Beatrice to Dante. No specimen of
Addisonian mockery could be more gentle, yet more
covertly penetrating, than this burlesque, in which the
erudite bird, after much reference to Aristotle, Plato,
and "other clerkis," sums up solemnly with the platitude
that "speche is soun, or elles no man mighte hit here."
There is a learned article by Rambeau, in which the

obligations of the *House of Fame* to the *Divine Comedy* are exhaustively enumerated. As we glance down the list of parallels collected in this article we find that in almost all of them Chaucer is putting in just a little touch of the ridicule which he elsewhere deals out to Geoffrey de Vinsauf or Bishop Bradwardine.

Again, when a maxim of Dante's (*Purg.* VII. 121) is put into the mouth of the Wife of Bath (*C. T. D* 1126), we must be dull if we do not see that Chaucer is applying once more the same humorous solvent as when portentous quotations from the Distichs of Dionysius Cato, or from Valerius Maximus, are made by Chanticleer to Pertelote. There are indeed few of the resources of the satirist which were not at the disposal of this consummate humorist; and this is one of the most familiar.

We have already indulged in conjectures as to Chaucer's opinion of Inferno; and they are tolerably well confirmed when we observe how in actual fact he deals with the place. Should an opportunity occur of describing it, he passes it by with a certain contempt. Aeneas, he tells us (*H. F.* 445), saw "every tourment in helle"; but to go through the list is far too tedious for Chaucer:

> Whoso willeth for to knowe,
> He moste rede many a rowe
> On Virgile, or on Claudian,
> Or Daunte, that hit telle can.

Similarly, his method of dealing with the great words over the portal of hell—words which, of course, he appreciated at their full worth and was far from wishing to ridicule—was to transfer them to the gate of a park (*Parl. Foules*, 122), where they are of considerably milder import than in their original position. As for the story of Ugolino, to which we have already referred, he robs it of its terror and leaves only the pathos. And even so, though it is prefaced by a definition of tragedy which might have been "conveyed" from Dante's letter to Can Grande, he allows the Knight and the Host to say of the series in which it occurs that a few more of such stories will be too much for them. "It is a peyne to here of hevinesse."

While on the subject of hell, then, Chaucer seems to have "held the opinion of all sensible men," an opinion which, as is well known, all sensible men keep to themselves; on Purgatory he is a little less reticent; but even here his views are interesting, more especially as he expresses them not as his own, but from behind the personality of Scipio Africanus:

> But brekers of the lawe, soth to seyne,
> And lecherous folk, after that they be dede,
> Shul alwey whirle aboute therthe in peyne;
> And then, foryeven alle hir wikked dede,
> Than shul they come unto that blisful place,
> To which to comen God thee sende his grace

(*Parl. Foules*, 78); where it is noticeable that he applies to Purgatory the words used by Dante of the second circle of Inferno (v. 33); as if indeed the "milder shades" were far more congenial to him than the eternal darkness. Of Heaven we have a fairly lengthy description in the account of the arrival of the "light ghost" of Troilus in the next world. But it is worth observing that in the parallel passage in the *Knight's Tale* on the death of Arcite, whether because Boccaccio's celestial lore had already been used or for some other reason, Chaucer refuses to say anything as to the abode of the departed paladin's soul. Unlike Dante, he cannot boast of having been in the next world, and will not talk about a place of which he knows nothing. The whole passage reads like an implied censure of some of Dante's sweeping judgments:

> His spirit chaunged house, and wente ther,
> *As I cam never*, I cannot tellen wher:
> Therfor I stinte, I am no divinistre;
> Of soules finde I nat in this registre;
> Ne me ne liste thilke opiniouns to telle
> Of hem, though that they writen wher they dwelle.

All he will say now is that he hopes Mars will guide the soul of Arcite just as before he had handed over to Mercurie the charge of that of Troilus. It is fairly plain that Chaucer had doubts where Dante had certainties, and shrank, with a mixture of humour and modesty, from the enormous confidence with which the grim Florentine settled the future fates of men he had, or even had not, personally known. His business, like Shakspere's, was not to judge or to condemn, but to observe and understand the frailties and virtues of mankind. He was very unlike a Spinoza, but he would have thoroughly agreed with what that great philosopher says of the writers who "bemoan, deride, despise, or, as

12-2

usually happens, abuse," the infirmities of men. "He," says Spinoza, "who succeeds in hitting off the weaknesses of the human mind more eloquently or more acutely than his fellows, is looked upon as a seer"; for himself, he labours "humanas actiones non ridere, non lugere, neque detestari, sed intelligere." With the omission of a single word Chaucer might have adopted this motto as his own; and he had certainly no wish to be one of those who, by the method Spinoza describes, earn the title of "seers."

Allied with this religious certainty in Dante is his political confidence. He has no doubt that he is right in his opinions, and that his opponents are morally the worst of men. He has his excuses, indeed: for he had undoubtedly been very badly treated by those opponents. But from a literary point of view the constant harping upon the fraud of Pisa, the vanity of Bologna, and the wolfishness of Florence, is a sad defect: it interrupts the hopefulness of Purgatory and the fruition of Paradise. In the one, Guido del Duca forgets his heavenward path to dilate upon the degeneracy of the Valley of the Arno; in the other, Cacciaguida seems to find nothing better to do than to add a lengthy appendix to Guido's discourse. Nay, it crosses the very love of Dante for Beatrice, and tinges his admiration for St Peter.

It did not fall directly in Chaucer's way to dilate on this point: but a measure of the worldly wisdom of Pandarus would have saved Dante (as it might have saved Milton in similar case) from the worst exhibitions

of the fault. At least it would have saved him from the
iterations that so weary readers. "For though," says
Pandarus (*Troilus*, II. 1030)—

> For though the beste harpour upon lyve
> Wolde on the beste souned ioly harpe
> That ever was, with alle his fingres fyve,
> Touche ay o streng, or ay o werbul harpe,
> Were his nayles poynted nevre so sharpe,
> It shulde maken every wight to dulle,
> To here his glee, and of his strokes fulle.
> Ne iompre eek no discordaunt thing yfere,
> As thus, to usen termes of phisyk;
> In loves termes, hold of thy matere
> The forme alwey, and do that hit be lyk.

Chaucer, then, saw that this amazing confidence
shown by Dante in undertaking a task only possible to
absolute omniscience was due to his defect in the saving
quality of humour. But he was willing also to recognise
the influence of the same deficiency in less important
matters. No satirist that ever lived, for example, could
teach Chaucer a lesson as to solemn ridicule of irrelevant
learning. It has, indeed, been maintained that the whole
Nun's Priest's Tale is nothing but one long laugh at
pedantry. Exaggerated as this view may be, there can
be little doubt that Chaucer was inclined to make fun
not only of other people's displays of erudition but of
his own. Like all medieval writers, he loved to show
off, but, unlike most of them, he loved also to mock
at his little vanities. Hence it is not surprising that in
the tremendous list of authors whose works the Physician,
to the sad neglect of the Bible, had studied, occur

several names which in Dante appear in a serious connection. Thus we find in Limbo (*Inf.* IV. 141), Dios-
corides, Hippocrates, Avicenna, Averroes, and Galen,
all of whom, strangely enough, figure in the library of
the wonderful doctor of the Pilgrimage. But Chaucer
is certainly laughing at the doctor. It is plain, then,
that he is also laughing at Dante.

Another trick of medieval writers, and of Dante and
Chaucer among them, is their habit of telling the hour
by some astronomical paraphrase, rather than simply
and directly. Every note of time gave them a chance,
eagerly seized, of airing their scientific information.
Thus our Host sees well that the "yonge sonne" has
run more than a quarter of the arc of his artificial day:
and it takes him fourteen iambic pentameters to conclude that it is ten o'clock. Every reader of the *Divine
Comedy* could supply a score of parallels to the lore
of the Host: and, indeed, it is not hard to find good
excuses for both the innkeeper and the poet. But the
difference is that Chaucer was able to laugh at himself—
a feat which we may safely say that Dante never dreamt
of performing—and it is not hard to see that Chaucer
occasionally undertook the task for him. For, it appears,
Chanticleer was no less skilful an astronomer than either
of the instructed poets (*C. T. B* 4045):

> Wel sikerer was his crowing in his logge
> Than is a clokke, or an abbey horlogge.
> By nature knew he ech ascensioun
> Of the equinoxial in thilke toun;
> For whan degrees fiftene were ascended,
> Thanne crew he, that hit mighte nat ben amended.

And as a brief summary of his opinion on the habit generally, Chaucer, after a momentary lapse of his own, pulls himself up with the sarcastic words (*F* 1017):

> For the orisonte hath reft the sonne his light—
> This is as much to seye as hit was night;

thus in his humorous fashion untrussing in one breath himself, Dante, and the whole tribe of poetical pedants.

There are certain passages in the *Divine Comedy*, particularly in the *Inferno*, which it is difficult for the hardiest admirer to defend. Such are the miserable "flyting" between Sinon and Adam of Brescia—an episode borrowed from one of the feeblest of Horace's satires—the treatment of Filippo Argenti, and the still more unpardonable behaviour of the poet to Bocca. What Chaucer thought of these passages we have our means of guessing. He was not, of course, so greatly shocked by them as we are to-day. He was accustomed to the plain expression of hatred, both in deed and in word; nor is it certain that our present methods, though more discreetly veiled, are really more Christian. But the crudity of Dante was nevertheless too much for him; and he lets us see it. His "flytings" are quite as vigorous as those of Sinon and Adam; but they are between the Reeve and the Miller, or between the Summoner and the Friar: and, as we might expect, in their worst excesses they have a touch of humour which Dante's entirely lack, and which helps to redeem them in our eyes. A slight hint in the Prologue appears to us to make his view yet clearer. He tells us that he does

not know whether it was "by aventure or sort or chance"
that the lot fell on the Knight to give the first tale—
whereas it is clear that the accident was skilfully
engineered by the Host. But the words he uses are a
thoroughly Chaucerian parody of the line of Dante
(*Inf.* XXXII. 76):

Se voler fu o destino o fortuna;

in which the poet says that he is uncertain whether it
was by divine will, destiny, or mere chance that his
foot caught on the face of Bocca in the eternal ice of
Antenora. If this be the case, it is an additional indication of Chaucer's feelings, and shows that he, like the
majority of readers, had a low opinion of what is
probably the least pleasant passage in the whole of the
Divine Comedy. In a word, he shows towards his great
forerunner the attitude of Ben Jonson towards Shakspere: he loved the man, and honoured him as much
as any, but on this side idolatry.

XI

John Dryden

THIS is, alas! the last work of Dr Verrall's that we are likely to see[1]. That most acute and ingenious intellect, that most engaging and attractive personality, has passed from us, and practises its strength somewhere afar in the labour-house of being. No longer shall we hear that clear voice declaiming Tennyson or Shelley in its uniquely arresting fashion; no longer, except in memory, shall we look on that frail figure which was to us the very type of mind triumphant over pain. These twelve lectures on Dryden were the parting legacy which he made to us as Professor of English Literature in the University of Cambridge; and, if they had no other claim upon our attention, that sad interest of finality and irrevocability would nevertheless hold us for more than a brief while. But of course they have other claims. They are by Verrall—in other words, they contain many an illuminating criticism, many an arresting phrase, many a correction of old judgments, many a new judgment worthily advanced and carefully defended.

The lectures have been well edited by his widow, and all that could be done for them in the absence of the author's hand to add and to retouch has most certainly been done. Much, of course, that lent grace and impressiveness to the spoken word has inevitably been

---

[1] This essay was originally written as a review of Verrall's *Lectures on Dryden*.

lost: Dr Verrall did not confine himself to his manu-
script notes, but allowed himself almost the full freedom
of the extempore speaker; and, as with the Roman
orator immortalised by Tacitus, "Haterii canorum illud
et profluens cum ipso simul extinctum est." One lecture,
indeed, has been entirely omitted; it consisted simply
of a reading of the *Secular Masque*, with attention to
metrical effects, but without other comment. There is
much, also, of explanation, defence, and discussion,
which Dr Verrall would certainly have added to some
of these lectures, if he had lived to publish them himself.
To a literary student the most important point about
Dryden is his debt to his predecessors and his influence
on his successors; to this but a few pages are devoted,
and those not the most pregnant in the book. Again,
we have many noteworthy remarks on minutiae of metre
or phrase in individual poems, but there is no general
characterisation of Dryden as a poet or as a man of
letters—no such comprehensive criticism, for example,
as Professor Bradley or Dr Mackail would have given
us. There is no attempt to show how the man in Dryden
wrought upon the poet; and, though the criticism is
sympathetic—as all criticism ought to be—it is not
always, to our mind, profound or penetrating. Yet we
are grateful indeed to the pious hands which have
rescued these fragments from oblivion: we have learnt
so much from them that we would not by a single word
seem to cast scorn on such a gift. Three of the lectures,
in particular, seem to us of the highest value. One of
these, as might be expected, is on Dryden's *Essay of*

Dramatic Poesy. Here Dr Verrall's special gifts and knowledge have full play; this lecture contains by far the most illuminating account of the "Unities" that we have ever read. On the development of the English Ode, also, Dr Verrall has much to say that is both new and true; while the text of the *State of Innocence*, and of some other poems in a less degree, gives him opportunities for the exercise of his well-known gift of emendation. It could not but be that the art, so often tried upon the plays of Euripides, and even upon the novels of Jane Austen, should find room for its display in some of the works of Dryden. As readers of Mr Sargeaunt's Oxford edition of Dryden well know, few writers since the invention of printing stand in need of more careful collation and emendation than Dryden as generally printed; and Dr Verrall's attempts, successful or not, are warnings to us against the hasty and careless reading which assumes sense where there is none. But in all the lectures there abound the signs of a fresh and original mind. Verrall read Dryden, as he read everything, with his own eyes and not through the spectacles of commentators; and whatever he says, whether we agree with it or differ from it, is always a rebuke to laziness and a stimulus to active thought.

We confess, however, that, bearing in mind Dr Verrall's principles of taste as previously revealed, we are somewhat surprised at his admiration for Dryden as a poet. That a judge who could see the "too-much" even in Tennyson, should not have boggled more at Dryden, is a little astonishing. Dryden has of course his great

and surpassing merits. He was beyond doubt one of
the chief founders of modern English prose. After him,
the rhetoric of Jeremy Taylor, the stately periods of
Hooker, the majestic involutions of Milton, though they
might be imitated by a Burke, a Ruskin, or a Pater,
were bound to be left on one side by the ordinary writer.
He is the father of Addison, and through him the ancestor
of Goldsmith and even of Lamb. He is also, equally
beyond doubt, one of the very greatest "men of letters"
that England ever produced. Not Walter Scott, not
Swift, not Johnson, deserves that name more. Above
all, he has a representative character. This is a peculiar
character not always belonging to the greatest men.
Milton, for example, though the highest name in his
age, does not represent that age; and many other lofty
intellects, though *in* one epoch, are *of* another. But
Dryden has this character to a degree not equalled by
his successor Pope himself. Not for nothing did Gray
pass over Pope, and trace his own ancestry through
Dryden to the earlier masters; not for nothing did Keats,
seeking for a type of "heroic verse," model his *Lamia*
not on the *Temple of Fame* but on the *Fables*. Of the great
dynasty that ruled over English literature from 1660 to
1798, Dryden is the Hyder Ali, Pope only the Tippoo.

All this is true; but whether this character is sufficient
to qualify a man for the title of a great poet is another
matter. Thus to represent his age and country a man
needs, not the highest genius, but a multitude of second-
rate qualities remarkably developed and combined—
qualities which, in fact, rarely go with the highest

genius. Of all first-rate men, indeed, Goethe alone, perhaps, possessed them; while their possession, *without* the higher powers, enabled Voltaire to dominate French letters for sixty years. It was these qualities that met in Dryden, and they are fully sufficient, without our assuming his possession of any high creative power or imaginative insight, to account for his achievements and for his fame. He had an extraordinary power of assimilation; the ideas of his time he caught up almost before the time had recognised them, and his contemporaries, reading their own thoughts in his works, fancied him their inventor. He wrote plays in rhyme while rhyme was wanted; he abandoned rhyme precisely when it was about to cloy; he knew by a kind of instinct even the *words* that were just beginning to be popular, and seemed to know which were likely to be permanent; like his own Achitophel, he chose the winning cause and abandoned the losing with a skill that seemed almost uncanny. As a result, he remains for us the very type of the latter half of the seventeenth century. And herein lies his value to us. As was Tennyson to the Victorian Age, so was Dryden to the Caroline and the Jacobean; he who would know the time must know his Dryden. Dr Verrall justly lays stress on the "width" of Dryden's accomplishment in literature, and he quotes the weighty words of Gray in the *Progress of Poesy*, to illustrate and confirm his judgment:

> His less presumptuous car
> *Wide* o'er the fields of glory bear
> Two coursers of ethereal race.

All this is true; and we may admit it—with a change
of emphasis. Dryden had width, but he wanted depth.
He saw far, but he did not see below the surfaces of
things. And if this is the case, we must refuse him the
title of a great poet.

It is natural that critics like Dr Verrall, and to some
extent critics like Professor Raleigh, in their revulsion
from the contortions and sham profundity of the so-
called poets of to-day, should look back with longing
eyes to the sound commonsense of an earlier century,
in which we usually found reason, and if not reason,
at any rate rhyme. Precisely as the vapourings of some
Shaksperean critics have led to a reaction in favour
of Johnson's soberer view of Shakspere, so the wild
gymnastics of certain poets lead us to cry out for an
hour of Pope and Dryden. And we are right. Pope and
Dryden are better than bad poets, just as a sound wagon
is better than a faulty aeroplane. But whether they are
themselves poets or not is a question apart. To us, whatever be the definition of poetry—and on that we do not
propose here to wrangle—poetry without mystery is
not poetry at all. And of mystery we can find no trace
in Dryden.

It was long ago beautifully observed, that poetry, like
religion, deals with that which eye hath not seen nor
ear heard. In this sense John Wesley was right, when
he declared that poetry, to attain an imperishable
wreath, must be the handmaid of piety. It is therefore
not uninteresting to notice that Dryden's religion, such
as it was, was fully as destitute of mystery as his verse.

We are not here discussing whether his conversion to
Catholicism was genuine or not: we incline on the
whole to agree with Dr Verrall against Macaulay, and
to believe that within his limits Dryden was sincere.
But our point is that neither as Protestant nor as
Catholic does Dryden show any sense of the awfulness
of divine truth. In this aspect, as in others, he is the
representative of his age; and he who would understand
the kind of religion and the kind of theology from which
the later revivals have helped to deliver us, will find
the writings of Dryden a prime document. We are
struck everywhere in him by a curious lack of reticence
and reverence, by a total absence of awe, and indeed,
by that very familiarity in dealing with solemn matters
which it has been the habit of certain writers to find
in Puritanism alone. To Dryden Puritanism was utterly
abhorrent; but in him this familiarity is more obvious
and repellent than in any Puritan writer of our acquaintance. We need not look outside of Dr Verrall's
volume for our illustrations. Take, for example, the
Dedication of the *State of Innocence*—an opera which is
itself a very fair specimen of the want of reverence to
which we are alluding. Dryden thus addresses Mary
of Modena, Duchess of York: "Your person is so
admirable that it can scarce receive addition *when it
shall be glorified*"—a passage in which the flattery
borders very closely upon profanity. Nor does it stand
alone. As Dr Verrall reminds us, similar adulation is
ladled out in the *Eleonora* to the Countess of Abingdon
and to other virtuous ladies elsewhere. Of a piece with

these lapses are the verses in which Charles II, of all
people, is likened to the Almighty:

> So looks our Monarch on this early fight,
>   The essay and rudiments of great success,
> Which all-maturing time must bring to light,
>   While he, like Heaven, does each day's labour bless.
>
> Heaven ended not the first or second day,
>   Yet each was perfect to the work designed:
> God and kings work, when they their work survey,
>   And passive aptness in all subjects find.

In the prefatory note to *Annus Mirabilis*, written while
London was still smouldering under the ashes of the
Great Fire, the City Corporation is addressed as follows:
"You are now a phoenix in her ashes, and, as far as
humanity can approach, *a great emblem of the suffering
Deity*." God, he says, in the same passage a little lower
down, cannot destroy a virtuous nation, whatever He
may do to a virtuous man; for "Providence is engaged
too deeply, when the cause becomes so general." That
is, man would have a just complaint against God if He
allowed a great calamity, but not if He allowed a small
one.

It is this familiarity which accounts for the strange
descents into blasphemy that startle us so often in the
midst of passages otherwise unobjectionable. Lord
Howard of Escrick, in prison, received the Sacrament
in a mixture called lamb's wool; Dryden's allusion is
as follows:

> And canting Nadab let oblivion damn,
> Who made new porridge for the Paschal Lamb.

Of the Whig Sheriff, Slingsby Bethell, we are told,

> When two or three were gathered to declaim
> Against the monarch of Jerusalem,
> Shimei was always in the midst of them:

a blasphemy due, we trust, rather to a failure of memory than to intentional irreverence.

These passages have probably already wearied and shocked the reader; but it would be easy to multiply their number many times over. Incidentally we may observe that they neither wearied nor shocked their contemporary readers. Mary of Modena was a pious woman; but she made no objection to the gross bad taste—to use the mildest name—of the Dedication. Similar passages might be found everywhere in writers far removed from Puritanism. Similar lightness of tone slightly deforms even Ben Jonson's beautiful epitaph on Salathiel Pavy; similar profanity often scandalises us in the Catholic Pope. But in Dryden it marks not merely a lack of religious instinct, but also a prosaic cast of mind, which reveals itself not only in regard to religion, but equally in his way of approaching other lofty or mysterious subjects, which usually excite awe in the beholder and a certain restraint in the describer. Thus, for example, in the first *Ode on St Cecilia's Day*, he begins with the famous passage assigning the origin of all things to harmony; a passage which, despite the inevitable comparison with Milton's *At a Solemn Music*, it is possible to admire. But, ere the end, comes the usual bombast:

> Orpheus could lead the savage race,
> And trees unrooted left their place,

> Sequacious of the lyre;
> But bright Cecilia raised the wonder higher;
> When to her organ vocal breath was given,
> An angel heard, and straight appeared,
>   *Mistaking earth for heaven.*

So, too, in the almost equally famous ode to the memory of Anne Killigrew, we light pretty early on the banal lines:

> Cease thy celestial song a little space;
> Thou wilt have time enough for things divine,
> Since heaven's eternal year is thine;

and as we proceed we find

>   No ignoble verse,
> But such as thy own voice did practise here,
> While yet a young probationer,
>   And candidate of heaven.

Not less characteristic is the well-known bathos in the *Epitaph on Lady Whitmore*:

> Rest in this tomb, raised at thy husband's cost.

It does not need the example of the pious and high-minded Southey to prove that a Poet Laureate, however gifted and religious he be, may run very near to stupidity and profanity when a court funeral ode is demanded by his employers; but Dryden's *Threnodia Augustalis* almost rivals the "gouty hexameters" of the *Vision of Judgment* in the extraordinary style of its treatment of so solemn a theme as death:

> The Sons of Art all Med'cines try'd,
> And every Noble remedy applied,
> With emulation each assay'd
> His utmost skill, *nay, more, they pray'd.*

Never was losing game with better conduct plaid.
Death never won a stake with greater toyl,
Nor e'er was Fate so near a foil:
But, like a fortress on a Rock,
Th' impregnable Disease their vain attempts did mock;
They min'd it near, they batter'd from afar
With all the cannon of the Med'cinal War.

A modern reader, stumbling on these passages, and
innumerable others like them, in a set of elegant ex-
tracts, might be inclined to put all this down to mere
lack of humour. But he reads further, and finds that
this same Dryden has written an *Absalom and Achitophel*
and a *MacFlecknoe*, from which, whatever may be
absent, humour assuredly is not. It would seem that
neither Dryden nor his contemporaries—or at least those
of his contemporaries to whom his works specially
appealed—saw any incongruity in comparisons between
Death and a dice-player, or between Charles II and the
Almighty. It is not lack of humour, but lack of the sense
of mystery, that accounts for these extraordinary lapses.

If anything can be regarded as approaching religion
in sanctity, it is beyond doubt Love, which has raised
to sublimity, for a time at least, such men as Lovelace
or Carew, and which in Spenser or Montrose blended
inextricably with religion itself. But in his love poems,
if such they can be called, Dryden shows no more sense
of solemnity than Prior himself. Of this the songs in
the plays are a sufficient proof. A large number of these,
indeed, are too gross to bear quotation; but even the
selection printed by Mr Sargeaunt will bear out our
statement. It is safe to say that with all their dexterity

13-2

of metre—and Swinburne's imitations have often not
surpassed them in this respect—they contain not a single
lofty sentiment, and scarcely a single delicate or dainty
touch. To Dryden the goddess of love is a vulgar Venus,
and her attendant is an earthly Cupid; of the rapture of
love he knows nothing, and he never soars above its
pleasures. To sum up, in the minds of Dryden and the
men of that time, whatever they may have called themselves, religion was a gross anthropomorphic materialism,
love an affair of the senses, and poetry a mere versified
prose. Of the whole world of shadows, of the divine
skirts "dark with excess of bright," of obstinate ques-
tionings of invisible things, of the light that never was
on sea and land, they knew nothing. To them the con-
secration was wanting, and, as a result, to them the
poet's dream was not vouchsafed.

It remains then to inquire what it is that has given to
Dryden his immense reputation and his length of days.
For, as Dr Verrall points out, it is more than two
centuries since he died, and he is still read and admired.
He will be a bold man who asserts that Tennyson's
renown will stand so long a strain. In a famous lecture
recently delivered, the suggestion for which was given
by this very book of Dr Verrall's, Mr Balfour has
drawn our attention once again to argument in verse,
and has tried to give reasons why Dryden and Pope
adopted rhyme in argument, and why subsequent writers
have dropped it. Of this *genre*, in our opinion, Dryden
is the supreme exponent, and—though Mr Balfour
seems to prefer the *Essay on Man*—*Religio Laici* is to

our mind the highest example. Those who doubt this
statement might do worse than compare it with the
Essay, reading the two in close connection, and studying
them with attention not to their purple passages, but
to their arrangement and convincing power. If this be
fairly done there can, we think, be no doubt about the
verdict. In the *Essay on Man* there is no true reasoning
from beginning to end, but only a very skilfully produced semblance of reasoning. In Dryden we feel that
we are advancing from point to point; in Pope we find
no marshalling of premises with a view to a conclusion,
but merely the clever repetition of single isolated pro-
positions. Now, though the power of reasoning is by
no means a sign of the poetic gift, it is not on that
account to be despised. It is one of the highest of
human capacities, nor were they altogether wrong who
regarded it as the very image of God implanted in men.
But, while the ornament of verse added to reasoning
aids its effect considerably, no addition of verse will
by itself transmute reasoning into poetry. Even the case
of Lucretius proves nothing to the contrary. The *poetry*
in Lucretius emerges precisely when he *ceases* to reason:
and his "grand other-world manner" adorns not argumentation, but assertion based upon vision. By resolve
he is a philosopher, but Nature has made him a poet,
and he cannot resist the natural impulse. With Dryden
the case is different. He knew that he could *argue* in
verse better than in prose, and he chose verse not
because he might at any moment slip into poetry, but
because he felt that his syllogisms went better if cast

in an apparently poetical mould. But Reason, to use his own admirable language, is

> Dim as the borrowed beams of Moon and Stars
> To lonely, weary, wand'ring travellers;

whereas poetry, like religion, reposes on intuitive certainties. Some consciousness of this is shown in the final words of Dryden's own preface:

> If any one be so Lamentable a Critique as to require the Turn of Heroique Poetry in this Poem; I must tell him... that the Expressions of a Poem designed purely for Instruction ought to be Plain and Natural, and yet Majestic.... The Florid, Elevated, and Figurative way is for the Passions; for Love and Hatred, Fear and Anger, are begotten in the Soul by shewing their Objects out of their true proportion ...but Instruction is to be given by shewing them what they naturally are. A Man is to be cheated into Passion, but to be reason'd into Truth.

What is true of *Religio Laici* is true of *The Hind and the Panther*—with a difference. There is no need to insist on the absurdity of the plot; nor is the absurdity made any less, as Professor Saintsbury seems to hint, by the fact that Dryden had many models for it. *Reynard the Fox*, *The Owl and the Nightingale*, the *Plowman's Tale* (once foolishly ascribed to Chaucer), Chaucer's own *Parliament of Birds*, and a score of other medieval parallels, exhibit this same absurdity of the Beast-Fable, with incongruities even worse than those of Dryden. Dryden, in fact, when he became a Roman Catholic, seems to have gone back to Catholic times for his inspiration. But, when the initial absurdity is allowed for; when we have once realised that it is not a panther but an Anglican Bishop that is speaking; when we substitute Burnet for the Buzzard and Father Petre for the Martin; then it is impossible not to admire the extraordinary skill of the reasoning, the vigour of the language, and the liveliness of the occasional passages of narrative. Doubtless it is these qualities that Mr Balfour admired; and, in recommending the practice of argument in verse to modern writers, doubtless he is covertly persuading many so-called poets of modern times to resign a task for which Nature has not fitted them, and take up a kind of work which, though lower than what they aim at, is infinitely higher than what they attain.

Of the advantages which the verse-form gives to Dryden there is little need to speak, as Mr Balfour has discussed them fully enough in the lecture to which we have alluded. Point, brevity, vigour, are all secured, and the recurring rhyme fixes the argument in the memory of the reader far more effectively than any prose. Mr Balfour is of course right in asserting that if Dryden had wished he could have argued his case without rhyme: no one better. But there is one advantage in the rhyme-form which Mr Balfour does not mention, which yet, probably was present to Dryden's mind as it certainly was to Pope's. Sophistry is easier, and its detection more difficult, in rhyme than in prose. Poetry deals more in concrete instances, and in selected examples; these, if *carefully* selected, may well serve to disguise the truth or hide falsehood. *Transition*, in fact, which is so important to a prose argument, may be almost passed over in "poetry." Just as in Gray's *Elegy*, or in an Ode of Horace, the connecting links are left to be supplied by the reader, so in *Religio Laici* or *The Hind and the Panther*, the "nice dependencies" of thought are by preference omitted. And, when the reasoning wears thin, when a weak point becomes too obvious, then a skilful debater like Dryden is glad to avail himself to the full of all the opportunities for prudent silence which his verse-form allows him. The *Hind*, in particular, exhibits many instances, to those who care to look, of this judicious reticence. And not least in the final aposiopesis—for the end is decidedly abrupt. As was long ago pointed out by Macaulay, the work shows that a great alteration in the views of Dryden, or rather of those who employed his talents for their own purposes, took place while *The Hind and the Panther* was being actually written. At first the Church of England is treated with tenderness and respect, and is exhorted to ally herself with the Roman Catholics against the Protestant Dissenters; but at the end, it is the Dissenters that are urged to aid James against the Church. Hence the sudden ending; for to go on might well have been embarrassing. Dryden was as ignorant as everyone else what would be the next step in the ever-shifting policy of James; and the poem was inconsistent enough already without the addition of yet another inconsistency.

On the extraordinary cleverness with which this difficult task—and a task indeed it was, set by rigorous task-masters—is accomplished, we need scarcely dwell.

It has been noted clearly enough by every com-
petent reader, and not least exactly by Dr Verrall and
Mr Balfour. But we must enter one protest. This piece
of sublime hackwork—as purely a party pamphlet as
Johnson's *Taxation no Tyranny*, or Swift's *Conduct of
the Allies*—dictated as it was by Government interests,
and executed at the behest of a faction, must not be
dubbed "religious." Not even *Religio Laici*, the origin
of which was more independent, and still less *The Hind
and the Panther*, can be called such in any adequate
sense of the word. There is some amateur theology in
both. There is something of what we may call political
ecclesiasticism—a blend of religiosity and the sense of
expediency. Both of them bear plain marks that the
author was writing with an eye to the main chance, and
talking of God with a glance at Mammon. This is not
Religion, and we are sorry that Dr Verrall should, even
accidentally, have seemed to countenance the use of
such a term in reference to such works. They are indeed
scarcely more religious than *Absalom and Achitophel* or
the *Medal*, and not a whit more so than the *Character
of a Good Parson*. Just as these works endeavoured
argumentatively to justify Dryden's *political* position,
to defend Toryism against Whiggism, Charles against
Shaftesbury, or the Non-juring parsons against Tillotson
and Sherlock, so the so-called "religious poems," in a
manner equally argumentative, defend Dryden's theological position—or rather the station he occupied at
the moment—against his theological adversaries. But,
unless Butler's *Hudibras* is sacred poetry, we fail to see

why the title should even implicitly be given to *The Hind and the Panther*.

Nevertheless, religious or not, these two poems remain the first and the best exemplars of that whole class of "poetry" to which the *Essay on Man*, Gray's *Alliance of Education and Government*, and, to a partial extent, such works as Young's *Night Thoughts* and Johnson's *London* belong. They are the pioneers and the models of a school. Still more is this true of *Absalom and Achitophel*, of which Dr Verrall gives a just and discriminating account. As he says, it is a mistake to call *Absalom and Achitophel* a satire: Dryden himself calls it simply a poem. It is rather an adaptation of the style set by Chaucer in his *Prologue*, with the added piquancy of personalities. In the *Prologue*, the characters are types; in the *Absalom* they are portraits. The result is that the poem bears the character of a kind of contemporary epic. In this respect it has never been excelled; nay, it has never been approached. Pope's *Satires* are mere daubs in comparison; for whereas Dryden's portraitures always carry some stamp of truth, Pope's are mere effusions of mendacious spleen. Yet Pope, in his way, was imitating Dryden; and a long line of successors followed in the path thus marked out. Johnson's picture of Charles XII is nominally Juvenal; it is really Dryden. Goldsmith's *Village Preacher* is Dryden again. Cowper's *Table Talk* is Dryden adapted to a moral and religious end—an end very different from that of *Absalom* or of *The Hind and the Panther*. Nay, anyone who to-day should begin portrait-painting in verse, would, by the mere compulsion of literary history, follow in the same path. For the characters drawn by Dryden are not to be confused with the ordinary caricatures of satirical versifiers. That of Zimri, for example, is carefully kept free from malicious exaggeration; and that of Achitophel is hardly more severe than that of a historian of to-day. It is no small matter to have started—or revived—a kind of writing which has had so numerous and admirable a progeny; and here Dryden is not only the first, but the best of the kind.

Closely allied with this is the catholicity of taste which enabled Dryden to welcome and to praise many writers of a style and talent widely different from his own. The famous saying about Milton—"This man cuts us all out, and the ancients too"—may or may not be genuine; but his opinion of Chaucer is certain, and is recorded in the immortal Preface to the *Fables*; while his opinion of Shakspere is expressed everywhere. And such was the receptiveness of his nature that when he admired a writer he imitated him. Directly and openly he imitated Milton in the *State of Innocence*, Chaucer in *Palamon and Arcite*, and Shakspere in *All for Love*: but the imitations are not confined to these acknowledged borrowings; they are to be found at intervals throughout his works. And, though they are of course often hardly to be distinguished from parodies, they yet served the purpose of keeping before Dryden's readers an ideal and a manner that might otherwise have been forgotten for the time. *Palamon and Arcite*, for instance, is not Chaucer, but it brought Chaucer's name and writings

to the notice of many who might otherwise have
neglected him: and every now and then it *is* Chaucer
despite Dryden. Thus Dryden's works, while often
exemplifying the worst points of the new style, provided
something of an antidote; it might almost be said of
them that while preaching the things of a lower region
they actually "allured to brighter worlds, and led the
way."

Again, Dryden's writings, if rarely "of ethereal race,"
are in the main sound specimens of the uninspired. And
herein lies their special value to-day. It is not granted
to many to be true and high poets; the vision and the
faculty divine are rare and capricious gifts of Providence
or fortune; and those who have them do not always
keep them. But clearness of thinking, sureness of touch,
correctness of versification, accuracy in the presentation
of the thought—these are gifts within the powers of
many men of no lofty genius, and are too valuable to
be squandered and lost in the search after the unattainable. We have to-day many who would do well to limit
their aims to an attempt after the homelier virtues of
Dryden, while leaving the useless struggle after a
Miltonic sublimity; we have, in fact, too many so-
called poets who show the contortions of the Sibyl
without her inspiration. To such we would recommend
a study of the works of Dryden, whose failures are a
sign-post warning us off from the faults of bombast,
and whose many successes show what can be done by
knowing one's own strength and keeping within it.

XII

The Literary Detective

IT will always, one may imagine, be pleasant to discover, or fancy one has discovered, the source of
some idea or phrase in the work of a great poet.
At any rate, people never seem to tire of tracing the
germs of passages in such authors as Virgil, Dante, and
Tennyson, or of marking how the tiny seed grew in
the mind of the poet until it took the form familiar to
us. It is a harmless pastime, "immeasurably," as
Macaulay might have said, "more humane than cock-
fighting"; and, if it has its pleasures, has also its en-
nobling pains. Few things are more annoying than, after
spending perhaps months, however lamely, in running
down an allusion, to find that another has stepped down
before you. The present writer has had his share both
of the joys and of the sorrows that beset the path of
the literary detective. Of the disappointments he feels
it more manly to say nothing; but he well remembers
the happy start with which he found the true original
of the first stanza of Gray's *Elegy* in the *Argonautica*
of Apollonius; and he recalls how pleased he felt when
he saw that Pope had been to the *Nosce Teipsum* of
Sir John Davies for one of the best known couplets
in the *Essay on Man*.

> The spider's touch, how exquisitely fine!
> Feels at each thread, and lives along the line,

says Pope. Davies, as might be expected, is less concise:

> Much like a subtill spider, which doth sit
>   In middle of her web, which spreadeth wide;
> If ought do touch the utmost thread of it,
>   She feels it instantly on every side.

No poet provides more opportunities for excitements of this kind than Milton, whose range of reading was so wide, and whose love of allusion was so keen, that the greatest scholar can never be sure he has exhausted the suggestiveness of the simplest of his paragraphs, while his originality was so strong that his countenance, "like richest alchemy," transmuted even borrowed lead to gold. He did not steal: he annexed and assimilated. No commentator can track him everywhere; and it is probable that the last scholiast will leave something undetected.

The very first lines of *Paradise Lost* are an example of Milton's royal rapacity. There can be no doubt that, while the idea of these lines can be found everywhere, the wording was suggested by Donne's *Divine Sonnets* (No. 9; Chambers's edition, I. 162):

> That tree
> Whose fruit threw death on else immortal us.

We read a little further, and we learn that Satan fell with his crew "nine times the space that measures day and night." Here we have Milton blending heathen with Christian mythology in quite medieval fashion. It is true that according to Caedmon, Lucifer was *three* days in falling—one of many indications that Milton had not read the *Genesis*. But in *Piers the Plowman* we are told that these who "lopen out with Lucifer in lotheliche forme"

> Fellen out in fendes liknesse *nyne dayes* togideres,
> Til god of his goodnesse gan stable and stynte:

and we know that in the Norse tales Hell was nine days from Asgard. "That is to say of Hermod," says Snorri in the story of Balder, "that he rode nine nights through dark vales and deep, so that he saw not until he came to the river Gjoll." Doubtless Milton was here mingling monkish authorities (who themselves derived from heathen tradition) with reminiscences of Homer and Hesiod, who also speak of nine days in this connection.

When we are told (line 73), that Hell is "as far removed from God and light of heaven as from the centre thrice to the utmost pole," we turn for elucidation to a curious passage in the *Doctrine and Discipline of Divorce* (*Prose Works*, III. 224), where Milton, speaking of the heathen philosophers, says: "To banish for ever into a local hell, whether in the air or in the centre, or in that uttermost and bottomless gulf of chaos, *deeper from holy bliss than the earth's diameter multiplied*, they thought not a punishing so proper and proportionate for God to inflict, as to punish sin with sin." We discover therefore, first, that Milton derived his measurements of the Universe from medieval tradition, and secondly, that his precision is no more to be taken literally than that of Dante. The real hell of Satan is to be found in that gradual deterioration which transforms him from the archangel ruined of the first Book to the crawling snake of the tenth.

In Book I (line 794), we are told that Satan, like Belshazzar, presides over a meeting of a thousand of his lords, while the churls and vassals throng without the hall. The hint for this seems to be found in Ovid (*Met.* I. 170 *sq.*)—a poet for whom Milton, like Dante and the medieval poets generally, had a great and perhaps undue regard:

> Dextra laevaque deorum
> Atria nobilium valvis celebrantur apertis.
> *Plebs habitant diversa locis.* A fronte potentes
> Caelicolae, carique suos posuere penates.

That Milton was well acquainted with Martial might be assumed as practically certain *a priori*; but it can easily be demonstrated from a survey of his prose writings. Thus in the First Prolusion (*Prose Works*, ed. Fletcher, p. 844), he quotes that "scitum et perurbanum Martialis,"

> Uxor pessima, pessimus maritus,
> Non miror bene convenire vobis.

In the *History of Britain* (*Prose Works*, ed. Bohn, v. 219), mentioning the well-known Claudia Rufina as of British birth, he says she "lived at Rome famous by the verse of Martial for beauty, wit, and learning" (cp. Mart. IV. 13, XI. 53):

> Claudia caeruleis cum sit Rufina Britannis
>   Edita, quam Latiae pectora gentis habet!
> Quale decus formae!

Again, in the *Defence of the People of England* (*Works*, I. 2, p. 349, ed. Fletcher), he quotes

O de Cappadocis eques catastis[1]

from Martial (x. 76). Nor are these the only indications that might be adduced to show that Milton knew both the language and the substance of the Epigrams: his Latin poems have reminiscences of the one, and his controversial works make tolerably frequent use of the other.

This being the case, it becomes extremely probable that the famous lines introducing the description of the building of Pandemonium (*Par. Lost*, I. 696):

And here let those
Who boast of mortal things, and wondering tell
Of Babel and the works of Memphian kings,
Learn how their greatest monuments of fame,
And strength, and art, are easily outdone
By spirits reprobate—

were suggested by the first epigram in Martial's *Liber Spectaculorum*—a book which, though not included in the *editio princeps*, is found in Gruter's edition of 1602. Notice how, later in the passage, Milton refers once again to "Babylon and great Alcairo," the latter of which he doubtless identified with Memphis; and the phrase "pendent by subtle magic" may have been sub-consciously due to the *pendentia* of the epigram:

Barbara pyramidum sileat miracula Memphis;
Assyrius iactet nec Babylona labor;
Aere nec vacuo pendentia Mausolea
Laudibus immodicis Cares in astra ferant.

[1] Milton reads *catastris*, unless this be a misprint in the edition

Such a reminiscence is precisely in the style of Milton, who loves to seize hold of words and phrases from the classics or from earlier poets generally, and give them a loftier application than was in the mind of those who originally employed them. Of this habit every reader can easily provide examples.

The magnificent description of the opening of Hell-gate (*P. L.* II. 880), with its unsurpassable onomatopoeic effects, may have been suggested by the vastly inferior passage in Lucan (*Pharsalia*, III. 153):

> Protinus abducto patuerunt templa Metello.
> Tunc rupes Tarpeia sonat, magnoque reclusas
> Testatur stridore fores—

lines which, as is well known, Dante imitated in *Purgatorio* (IX. 136). But how Milton has transformed them!

> On a sudden open fly,
> With impetuous recoil and jarring sound,
> The infernal doors, and on their hinges grate
> Harsh thunder, that the lowest bottom shook
> Of Erebus.

We are reminded of the words in *At a Solemn Music*, which tell how

> Disproportioned Sin
> Jarred against Nature's chime, and with harsh din
> Broke the fair music that all creatures made.

Once more, when in *Paradise Regained* (II. 13), we are told that the disciples of Christ, increasing in doubt as the days increased, thought sometimes that he might be "only shown, and for a time caught up to God," it is hard to resist the conviction that here Milton is recalling Virgil's famous words on the young Marcellus (*Aeneid*, VI. 869):

> *Ostendent terris hunc tantum fata*, neque ultra
> Esse sinent.

Compare further the later line "from what high hope to what relapse" with Virgil's

> Nec quisquam in tantum spe tollet avos.

Professor Summers, in his edition of Seneca's *Select Letters*, points out certain passages in Milton's works which seem to bear traces of Senecan reminiscence. These are *Paradise Lost*, XI. 504 (=*Marc.* 22. 3), and *Comus*, 362 (=*Epp.* 24. 1; 13. 10). He also adds that there is a very Senecan tone about *P. L.* VI. 171 *sq.*:

> Apostate, still thou err'st, nor end wilt find
> Of erring, from the path of truth remote.
> Unjustly thou deprav'st it with the name
> Of servitude, to serve whom God ordains
> Or Nature: God and Nature bid the same,
> When he who rules is worthiest, and excels
> Them whom he governs—

a "tone" which every reader of Seneca will recognise. Similarly, the famous passage in *Par. Regained*, IV. 320, while mainly directed *against* Seneca and the Stoics generally, has something recalling him:

> Who reads
> Incessantly, and to his reading brings not
> A spirit and judgment equal or superior,
> Uncertain and unsettled still remains.

Compare *Ep.* 84. 1: "cum ab aliis quaesita cognovero,

tum et de inventis iudicem et cogitem de inveniendis."
Similarly, *P. L.* IV. 774:

> Sleep on,
> Blest pair, and O yet happiest, if ye seek
> No happier state, and know to know no more!

seems to be a conflation of Virgil's well-known "For-
tunati sua si bona norint," and Seneca, *Ep.* 90 *ad fin.*:
"ignorantia rerum innocentes erant." Again, *Samson*,
1660 *sq.* may be a kind of answer to Medea's arguments
(*Medea*, 431): "trahere cum pereas libet"; while *P. L.*
X. 762, as well as the passage already quoted (*P. L.* XI.
504), bears some resemblance to *Medea*, 507: "Ingrata
vitast cuius acceptae pudet." Compare especially, "if
we we knew what we receive would either not accept
life offered, or soon beg to lay it down."

But after all one need not be a scholar to feel and say
such things as these; and not everyone who utters a
pessimistic platitude is quoting from a weeping philosopher.

For EU product safety concerns, contact us at Calle de José Abascal, 56–1°, 28003 Madrid, Spain or eugpsr@cambridge.org.

www.ingramcontent.com/pod-product-compliance
Ingram Content Group UK Ltd.
Pitfield, Milton Keynes, MK11 3LW, UK
UKHW020317140625
459647UK00018B/1913